Short's Stories

Short, Ronan
Short's Stories: Moose Dropping
Volume 4: A 'Stopover' in Alaska, 1966–1968
978-0-578-31049-7

1. Biography & Autobiography / Memoir.
2. History / United States / 20th Century.

For more information, contact the author at ronanshort@hotmail.com

Printed in the U.S.A.
Distributed by Ingram

Cover: Here I am, a real *haole*, in Aloha land.

SHORT'S STORIES

Volume 4
Moose Dropping

A 'Stopover' in Alaska
1966–1968

RONAN SHORT

Short's Stories

For

Keenan Charles
Gillian Klara
Jack Douglas
Rose Esperanza
Finn Endicott
David Maria
Charlotte Endicott
Henry Parker
Kinzley Francesca
Carmella Jo
Oliver Gray
Isla Grace

Not all are related, but all are loved.

The past is never dead. It's not even past.

—William Faulkner

Encounter With
my First Alaskan

I had stepped off the Pan Am flight from Seattle to Tokyo for a brief stopover in the refueling location. It was mid-August in Fairbanks as I strolled around the almost-deserted terminal and by the time I picked up my luggage, my bags were the only two left on the platform. I stepped outside and was standing on the curb when I observed a Disneyesque moose raise his head from the pond and disappear as with the *wind in the willows*.

I realized then that I had landed in a part of America that really wasn't a part of America. It was Alaska.

"Hey buddy! You goin' to town?"

I looked around and saw an old tan pickup truck with lumber and *stuff* piled haphazardly in the back. Thinking the driver was talking to somebody on my left, I ignored him. I then glanced in that direction and saw no one.

The driver repeated his exhortation and added, "Yes, you! I haven't got all day you know." I pointed at my chest and he curtly responded, "Yes! No one else, is there?"

I nestled my luggage on top of all his *gear* in the back of the truck and climbed in.

"First time here, is it?" he said.

"Actually," I replied confidently, "I'm not coming here at all. I'm just passing through for the weekend."

"Yeah, that's what we all say. I've been here twenty years now; can't seem to find the road out of town, or get myself on an airplane." he smiled.

'Where are you staying?' he asked.

"Don't know yet," I replied weakly.

We rattled down the two-lane Airport Way into town and turned left onto Cushman Street, then right onto First Avenue just before the rather new-looking bridge over the Chena River.

We pulled up by the Fairbanks Chamber of Commerce building. It was a single-story log structure, complete with a live and growing sod roof. The driver was looking the other way though, across the street.

"There, the Steel Hotel," said the man. "You'll be fine. They rent rooms by the hour! Just kidding, some of my family that I rarely see own the place. You should be fine."

Should be? I retrieved my gear and thanked him for the ride. "Is it dodgy here?" I added.

"Don't know that word," he replied, "but this place, this whole place gets *a-hold* of you."

I just smiled. I was leaving for good in two days time.

I'm unsure if I ever saw that man again. I didn't get his name, and wondered if he ever saw me, but I was to see his smile, jovial welcome, and helpfulness in a thousand faces in the coming years.

The Steel Hotel was borderline, but safe and not a lot of noise.

"No women in the room after nine p.m.," admonished the desk clerk.

"But I can have two in there at eight-thirty," I replied, jokingly.

It was not well received. "You college types should stay up at the end of College Road."

"What's there?"

"There's what they call a *university*. About three miles away by road, and a million from the town down here."

MOOSE DROPPING

The hotel rooms there were cheap, about four bucks a night, but the walls were, too. They were made of one sheet of worn, noisy plywood. *Half-inch CDX* was the nomenclature I would later learn by heart. There was a wash basin in the room and a cracked mirror...or was it the other way round? Anyway, the toilet and shower were down the hall. I took a shower and headed out for a walk around the downtown area.

First Avenue then was lined with dilapidated bars made of either worn logs or even more worn painted-frame construction. Most had *false fronts* and an implied second story that just held a wall and windows, some with colorful painted figures and faces in them. On the river side was the USO building, a sort of social club for GIs from the two military bases nearby. I turned right past a new car dealership and right again on Second Avenue. I was now met, and totally bemused, by an array of bar signs interrupted only by a movie house, a hotel, and in the distance, the post office and courthouse building.

The first bar of note was Tommy's Elbow Room, later to become a major college hangout. Opposite it was the joyless Chena bar, then the Savoy Hotel, most unlike the namesake in London and Paris both for its décor and clientele. Then at the end of the block was the bar with the unusual and possibly most controversial name ever—The Mecca Bar. What made that name even worse was its subtitle—*The Mirrored Mecca*, a further insult to Islam and its ban on human image representation.

Across Cushman Street at the end of the block stood the federal building; this five-story edifice housed the post office, IRS offices, courtrooms, and the downtown jail. On the back side was an outdoor mezzanine platform that, according to the late Ted Lowell, a former US marshal and family friend, held gallows that had hanged several convicted prisoners.

Day Two and a Job

The sun was up and dragging the day with it. I ambled over the Cushman Street Bridge past Samson's Hardware and the International Hotel, aka the Big I bar—famous then, and even more so now. I passed the *News-Miner* newspaper building and headed up Illinois Street toward College Road and the *halls of higher learning.*

At the top, I turned left and the traffic increased a bit so I thought of hitchhiking. It was only the third or fourth car—a black Plymouth Valiant as I remember—that eased to a stop. I got in and the first thing that greeted me was the smile and handshake of a guy whose name turned out to be Ted Anderson. We drove through the subdivision of Lemeta and as we drove on up College Road he explained that he worked at the materials testing lab of the state highway department located in the basement of the Duckering Building on the University of Alaska campus. He dropped me off there and suggested that I go up a couple of floors and look at all the undersea three-dimensional marine maps of the world's oceans that lined the hallway of the Institute of Marine Science (IMS). I arranged to meet him at five o'clock, as he had kindly invited me to sleep on his couch, which meant I could check out of the *expensive* hotel. Ted turned out to be an accomplished musician, playing not only the guitar and banjo, but the bagpipes as well; he came from a Scottish immigrant family in Idaho and had been in Alaska for several years.

Upstairs was a long corridor of offices and labs, the walls of which, as Ted had promised, were covered in maps of the world's oceans in 3-D relief. I was fascinated and walked around for about an hour studying it all, from the mid-Atlantic ridge to the Marianas Trench, when a voice behind me said, "I've been watching you from my office. You're really intrigued with it all, aren't you? Would you be interested in a job?"

"Oh no," I quickly replied, "I'm only here for a couple of days."

The voice belonged to a guy named George. He was the business manager for IMS.

"I'm off to Tokyo when the Pan Am flight comes through again," I added.

"We could use someone now," said George, "to help run the mass spectrometer and also go out as a technician on oceanographic cruises. And Pan Am? They're here all the time."

I was about to exclaim with further *no's* when I realized that I had one twenty dollar bill left and a pocket full of *shrapnel*.

"Let's talk in my office," said George, and disappeared.

When I was guided through to his office I also met Vera Alexander, who was a Ph.D. graduate of the university and the faculty member I would work for. I was offered, and accepted, a temporary job as a Marine Technician ll; the salary was $750 dollars a month, almost double what I had made at Geigy in New York, a princely sum indeed for 1966. I started a few days later and Ted Anderson and I took an apartment together on College Road.

After several days of instruction and practice, I was reasonably competent on the mass spectrometer, and let loose to run a big backlog of samples. A *mass spec* is a machine that measures the mass-to-charge ratio of ions. A sample, solid or liquid, is heated then passed through a vacuum tube and read by a computer. It can perform this function with simple or complex molecules and is now in common use in airports to detect explosives and other chemicals illegal to transport on aircraft. Ours, then, was a machine that filled a large lab with electronic systems linked with an extensive array of lab glassware all connected into one system. Nowadays a mass spec can fit into a large suitcase.

A Russian Poet
Comes to Fairbanks

Several guest visitors appeared at the Fairbanks campus that fall of 1966. The first I saw was a female author, name forgotten, who was met by Ed Skellings at the airport. What I do remember is that soon after arriving she greatly tarnished her entire visit by announcing to all within earshot: *I've always wanted to come to Alaska, ever since I wrote a book about it!*

Having *blotted her copy book*, as we British say, that mistake made her visit less than spectacular, but the following visitor to the campus that year came thundering in accompanied by several odd entourages.

We had all heard around the Student Union Building (SUB) that a visitor from far away was soon arriving to give readings and lectures. We, or at least, I, assumed it was a British or Irish writer of some repute, but the first signs we all saw were almost unnerving.

Tall men with very short haircuts were observed in the hallways of the Bunnell Building, standing at the back of lectures in Schaible Hall, and sitting in small groups in the only other main campus auditorium—the Duckering Building.

Finally Sarkis Atamian, an Armenian-born sociology professor, spat out with disgust, *Russians—they're Soviets! What the hell they're doing here, I don't know!*

7

SHORT'S STORIES

A day or so later, Bud Powell, the head of the local FBI office, was pointed out to us in the SUB. He was having coffee with two or three men in dark suits and short haircuts; these guys were speaking with regular American accents.

Soon after these sightings, Skellings strode into the SUB, surrounded by several of the aforementioned *suits*, accompanied by a tall, slender man with blond hair and arresting eyes.

The man in question was Yevgeny Yevtushenko, the famed dissident Russian poet—a man adored by most people in Russia and watched with wary concern by Kruschev and the other Soviet leaders. He was on a *non-public* reading tour of the US sponsored by Queens College, New York, and was nearing the end in Alaska. He had already been taken down the Richardson Highway almost halfway to Delta to visit the well-known Alaska poet John Haines at his homestead.

I was introduced to him by Ed Skellings as an English graduate student and a new poet. Stunned by the compliment, I said nothing.

But he said, "Oh, English eh? You drink lime juice! I'm almost out."

"Jawohl," I replied—in German—well, I didn't know any Russian.

He was not amused, but moved on with, "Can you get me some? I have plenty vodka, but I could use some lime juice. And please, call me *Zhenia*.".

"Of course," I replied, "but Zhenia, you cannot buy any alcohol around the U, but Lindy's grocery here always has Rose's Lime Juice. I'll get some."

His readings and workshop were exciting and raucous, with Yevtushenko reciting several poems, and as a finale, a section of his well-known epic, "Babi Yar," that told vividly of the brutal mass killings of Jewish refugees that began in 1941. The publication of the poem in 1961 in a literary magazine had become a thorn in the Soviets' side, and they watched him closely. These murders, eventually totaling 100,000 Jewish

"Ronan, can you get me some lime juice?"

people, by the Soviet regime had taken place in a large ravine outside the city of Kiev. It was an emotional evening and during it I had my first inkling that perhaps I could put some of my experiences and thoughts down on paper.

As I recall, it took almost an hour for us all to get into Schaible Hall as we had to line up and get vetted and approved by the FBI, the KGB, and the Secret Service.

We had some clandestine cocktails afterward in Skellings' office—with lime juice, of course. A short time later, a group of us, including Zhenia, evaded the various *minders* and in several vehicles headed downtown to the popular Tiki Cove to eat. As word spread, the basement Asian restaurant got too crowded so we left and drove over to the Boatel Bar on Airport Way. This was the original *Boatel*—not the present cement block structure, but an actual vessel moored on the banks of the Chena River that was converted into a bar/nightclub.

One of Zhenia's expressions to all of us was, *Don't die before you're dead.* He titled a book with that later.

SHORT'S STORIES

I never actually saw Yevtushenko again, but felt a connection from our brief acquaintance. Years later, he came to the US and settled in Tulsa, Oklahoma with his family and taught at the university there. He died in 2017 at 84.

USSIAN POET VISITS U OF A — Russian poet Yevney Yevtushenko visited Fairbanks and the University f Alaska this week, and invited a group known as the Flying Poets" to visit him in Moscow next summer. Warfel and Dr. Edmund Skellings, of the university, Albert Todd, professor of Slavic languages at Queens College, New York, and Yevtushenko. The Flying Poets plan an over-the pole flight to Russia.

Russian poet Yevgeny Yevteshenko visited Fairbanks and the University of Alaska this week and invited a group known as The Flying Poets to visit him in Moscow next summer. Here discussing the trip are Ken Warful, Ed Skellings, Albert Todd, and the Russian poet. (Photo: *Fairbanks News-Miner*, December 1, 1966)

The Flying Poets planned an *over-the-pole* flight to Russia, but it never happened.

CRUISING AROUND ALASKA

By early December of 1966, Ted Anderson had joined IMS, and was also working for Vera Alexander. Soon, we were both sent off to Juneau on our first oceanographic cruise. The ship was the RV *Acona*, a ninety-foot research vessel owned and operated by the university, and permanently based in Juneau. It had a crew of about six, plus a faculty member/ chief scientist. On this cruise, graduate student Peter McRoy had his own experiments to carry out with us, the technicians.

What lies beneath?

The cruises in the summer were usually in the calmer waters of Lynn Canal, Icy Strait, or Frederick Sound, but as winter set in that year we headed out for the southern area of Chatham Strait.

On this winter outing, we turned into a narrow channel to sample a pre-arranged station. We stood on deck in the biting cold, the wind whipping under our coats. Jack, the deckhand, flashed a wry smile to Kenny on the bridge and went below.

The next thing we heard was the soaring notes of Joan Baez filling the air. We smiled and started to get to work, but Jack said to wait.

Captain Ken Turner at the helm of the *RV Acona*, gazing through the Kent 'clear-view screen' Spinner.

"Look, there's a seal," I yelled. "Oh, another—holy shit, there's hundreds!"

Everywhere we looked, seals popped up and down as Joan's soaring notes progressed. When the tape finished, we were all laughing, and then the last seals and sea lions disappeared below. We sampled the station with big smiles, went below deck, and played the tape again for ourselves.

The method of taking water samples on research vessels is done using Nansen bottles; these are glass tubes encased in metal that are suspended on a cable that is lowered down to pre-determined depths. The bottles are open, and when the cable stops at the correct depth, a weight is passed down the line to trigger the closing of the bottles. This captures water samples at the correct depth for later analysis in the onboard lab.

The *Acona* had departed sunny cold Juneau on an early December morning. The vessel steamed down Stevens Passage, across Frederick Sound where we stopped at different *stations* to take samples, and entered Chatham Strait at about the middle of its 150-mile length.

The seas were only about two to three feet, but as Kenny Turner, the skipper, said with a warning finger, "They're building though, and by the time we get to Cape Ommaney we'll all be needing our rain gear." And he added, "This *Terra Softa* today ain't gonna be very softa!"

It was several more hours before we steamed passed the islands at the mouth of the Cape, with the waves now at about four to six feet. Wind, clouds, and rain were now the order of things as we ploughed into ever increasing waves in the Gulf of Alaska. After two hours, the seas were at eight to ten feet, but we were close to our station. A few minutes later, the steel sampling platform was swung out from the deck and I stepped on, grasping the handrail. I had full rain gear on with a hood and long rubber gloves. I had attached several Nansen bottles from the rack on the platform and was hurriedly working with both hands occupied when the large wave hit.

I reached out, in error of course, to grab a cable near the rail, but it swung away from me and I missed. Falling back, I grasped at the platform uprights and missed again as the green water loomed above. The wave engulfed me and the entire platform.

I was soaked to the skin, my boots were full. I grasp for something solid, but there was only a wall of icy cold green water. After an eternity of flailing around, I felt a firm yank up under my raingear jacket and around my suspenders. I was pulled down with a slam. Jack, the deckhand, a long-time commercial fisherman and tugboat captain, had seen it all going down, literally, had jumped forward from the cable controls, and thrust his arm up under my flapping jacket to grasp the suspenders.

"You owe me a beer. Make that two," was all he said, as I sputtered back some damp vowels from my water-soaked brain.

Ted Anderson took my place and I sloshed below decks to my bunk and peeled off the wet clothes, wringing cups of water out of my t-shirt and socks. By the time I reappeared on deck to help as needed, I was just in time to see Ted get soaked. We realized the waves were now formidable.

It was only moments later when Kenny the skipper announced over the PA system that the station was being abandoned due, as he put it, tongue firmly in cheek, "to the brief arrival of a slight breeze and some wavelets."

The vessel turned about with some difficulty as the seas built rapidly to about fifteen to eighteen feet. We reduced speed to just a few knots and headed slowly back toward Cape Ommaney. Several of us crowded onto the bridge to watch the spectacle. The bow of the *Acona* ploughed deep into each wave as the wall of green water rose up and slammed against the steel bridgework and the windows.

Kenny the skipper explained that this was the real danger. This green water—a solid wall of a big wave—could hit the bridgework and cause glass breakage, loss of electrical controls, steerage, or possibly worse for the vessel.

I was now experiencing waves of a different kind in my stomach and went quickly below decks to my bunk, only to rush to the head nearby and start vomiting. This was followed eventually by the dry heaves. After a while, I rummaged through my kit bag and swallowed some Dramamine tablets—a big mistake. I was now a semi-comatose, slightly nauseated person and totally useless for anything on the remainder of the voyage.

It was several hours before Coronation Island came into view a distance off the starboard bow and after we passed it, the wave height dropped and the seas lay down as we turned into more calm waters of Chatham Strait.

Two days later, we moored up again in Juneau. The samples had been stabilized in the lab and Ted and I ran them when we were firmly tied to...*Terra Firma*!

There were a few more *cruises* on the *RV Acona*. A few years later, she was cut in half and twenty feet or so of lab and research space was added. This also gave more stability during periods of *wavelets*. Years after that, she was sold off and replaced by another vessel, the *Alpha Helix*, that was then based in Seward.

RV Acona tied up safely with barely a wavelet.

FIFTY BELOW ZERO

AND THE NUCLEAR OPTION

It was a cold night in Fairbanks in January of 1967: forty-eight below zero and going down. My roommate Ted and I were cozy and warm in our apartment on College Road. We had beer, a small joint to smoke, a black and white TV, and possibly two female grad students would swing by on their way and take us to Tommy's Elbow Room. Then the phone rang. It was our boss, Vera Alexander....

It turned out that earlier that day she had driven down to Fort Greely, near Delta Junction, with a certain Dr. Mary Belle Allen, who had been, in the early forties, a young, attractive and very accomplished scientist in the biological sciences from Los Alamos National Laboratory in New Mexico.

Due to her brilliance, she was personally recruited by Robert Oppenheimer himself to join the Manhattan Project, the top-secret US effort to create the atomic, and later, hydrogen bombs. Massive nuclear engineering labs were built at Oak Ridge, Tennessee and Hanford, Washington, with testing done at several sites, including New Mexico and the Nevada Test Site near Las Vegas. Dr. Allen worked for many years for the Atomic Energy Commission (AEC). By the time she arrived to work at the Institute of Marine Science (IMS), however, she was a very grouchy, overweight, middle-aged woman with a strong appetite for alcohol.

The two women had been invited to Fort Greely that cold day in January to give a talk and receive an award from AEC officials. They had driven down in the afternoon in Vera's car for an early dinner appointment and an awards ceremony at the Officer's Club. The reason Fort Greely was chosen was the little known fact that there was a small nuclear reactor there and the AEC officials had come to check it out. It's still there today in a decommissioned state—the only one in Alaska. It is codenamed the SM1-A, and is attached to the regular power plant.

The dinner and talks went well and by the time the conferring of a medal on Dr. Allen came, she was quite inebriated and rapidly adopting a sour disposition. The weather had also deteriorated further, with blowing snow adding to the extreme cold. That is when Vera called our phone and brought a rapid end to the cozy evening with a small TV, possibly the co-eds and Tommy's Elbow Room, etc.

Vera requested that we go to the university and get the International Scout that belonged to IMS; it had a high clearance for snow and a good functioning four-wheel drive.

We pulled on our worn Air Force *mukluks* and Army surplus parkas and mittens. We drove up College Road to the Duckering Building on campus and switched out Ted's old Plymouth Valiant with the Scout in the IMS garage. Carrying the six pack, now down to four, we headed out through the downtown ice fog and on down the Richardson Highway. The sky was gun metal grey—no, that was still just the ice fog, close to the ground and about thirty feet high. It soon petered out with the traffic and we were on the road to Delta Junction, almost a hundred miles away. The highway in those days was quite narrow and with more hills than today. We made slow, steady progress on the highway, but more rapid progress on the beer, so our supply was increased at the Salcha Store.

We arrived on post at about nine p.m. and were quickly directed to the Officers Club, where our *charges* were waiting impatiently at the entrance. Getting them both ensconced in the back seat of the Scout took longer. We departed, and the first dozen miles or so was relatively uneventful, except for the horizontal thirty mph wind. Then the rear heater, which we had not used so far, began to act up. At first the fan stopped, and then the heat faltered. Soon after we crossed the Tanana River Bridge, the heater in the front began to put out only lukewarm air and the windshield started to fog over. Ted pulled over near the narrow Quartz Lake turn off, jumped out, and opened the rear tailgate to howls of complaints from the occupants. He grabbed a piece of cardboard and some wire among the junk in the back, as I got out. The two of us then quickly opened the hood and tied the cardboard against the front of the radiator, covering almost all of it.

"What on earth will that do?" I asked. It was my first winter in Alaska after all. I had no idea what we were doing.

"Get in" he shouted, not willing to discuss the high-tech improvements just then, "before we die!"

"Die!" erupted a loud voice from Madam Nuclear herself. "We're going to die!"

Ted just shook his head and drove off. After a mile or so, warmth, followed by heat, began to envelope us. Ted explained that the cardboard blocked the extreme cold, which had the added effect of a chill factor due to our speed, and cooled down the radiator.

"We must now watch the temperature gauge carefully," he warned. "If it gets really hot in here—"

"It will be wonderful," two voices whined in unison from the back seat.

"No, it won't," said Ted. "We'll have to stop and cut a small trap door in the cardboard to allow more cold air in." Low moans from the rear.

We drove on for an hour or so, finally arriving at the historic Richardson Roadhouse, originally constructed when this highway was part of the Fairbanks-Valdez Trail. We pulled in, parked, and entered to warmth, lights, and hot drinks. Mary Belle was already warmed all over thanks to her extra large hip flask. The rustic roadhouse had many signs behind the bar. The most well-known read: *There is no place like this place, anywhere near this place, so this must be the place!*

The engine did not overheat, but our two occupants did. They boiled over incessantly about it taking too long, and finally, when we arrived at Vera's house, Mary Belle clambered out and loudly announced in full meltdown, "Look, it's well after midnight! Now you've spoiled my Saturday as well!"

Ted and I drove straight over to the Switzerland Bar on Airport Way, had a night cap or three, and went home to bed.

The temperature stayed close to minus fifty, so we kept the Scout on Sunday and took the two female grad students— who finally appeared—out to lunch at Sam's Economy Café on First Avenue. They were impressed with the *government use only* vehicle plates, the free gas, and of course, the four-wheel drive, but even more impressed with the *free* food.

When we got to work on Monday morning, there was quite a *kerfuffle* going on at the Institute. Apparently, *someone* had left a private vehicle in the warm garage and the Institute Scout, a government vehicle with a full tank of government gas, was missing!

Bone Dropping

By the time spring days warmed the interior in 1967, Mary Henrikson, an art student I'd been seeing, had mentioned several times to me about going *out the Steese Highway* to old mining camps and looking for *stuff*.

This searching need of hers reared its head several times in the next year. In Ketchikan later that summer, she had me *collect* (meaning: drag out) what was left of two ancient Tlingit totem poles from their abandoned horizontal positions— rotting in the Tongass National Forest. With caution, while Mary kept repeating, *careful please, they're valuable*, I later carried them up two flights of loose, rickety stairs and following her guidance, placed them carefully across the ceiling joists in a friend's dusty unfinished attic. Apparently, many years later they were returned back to the tribe—accepted with ceremony and gratefulness.

So up the Steese Highway we drove on a Sunday morning, borrowing Ted Anderson's car, and headed up to Pedro Dome, about forty-five minutes away. We passed through the old mining community of Fox, with its striking vistas of *tailing* piles from the gold dredges. The dredges were enormous, four or five stories high, with a large steel bucket line on one end and a conveyor belt *tail* that distributed the waste, the tailings,

20

out to the sides on the other end. These imposing, weighty structures actually floated on their own ponds that the bucket lines created.

We drove on and stopped at the top near the Cleary Summit ski hill, the only one in the country then, where you drove to the top of the hill, parked, and skied down. *One free run*, the grizzly, bearded operator in the A-frame used to say with a chuckle. *If you don't have a rope tow ticket you can't come back up!*

It was then that Mary uttered a line that I've repeated to visitors from around the world whom I've taken to that spot. "If you start out walking from here," she said wistfully, looking north and pointing slightly to the right, "the odds are that you will not encounter another human being before you reach the North Pole—and that's at least a thousand miles."

She took in the view. I took in the view, especially the sight of her long straight blonde hair flicking up in the breeze, then we drove down the long hill toward Chatanika. As we neared the bottom of the hill, Mary produced a hand-drawn map and suddenly said, "*Ooh.* Turn right here."

There was nothing but brush and trees, and a small snow berm.

"Wait, wait, no. Now, here," her voice terse, but not bossy.[*]

There in a small gap in the willows and the ploughed snow berm was a tiny gravel turn-off that went back and down quite steeply. I cranked the wheel of the borrowed vehicle and bumped slowly down, headed toward what was marked on her map as, *Cleary City pop. 5,000 in 1906.*

The gold is all gone now, of course is a line that people here say all the time. Actually, no, that's quite false; the hills around Fairbanks are still full of gold, tons of it, but most in the *placer* form—tiny, almost microscopic flakes.

About twenty-five years ago, an international mining company, Kinross Gold, that had slowly acquired many gold claims on the south side of Pedro Dome, started an enormous

---

[*] Personal note to her niece, Jami, in Ketchikan!

open pit placer mining operation, named *Fort Knox*, and is still today a thriving concern with large profits. The massive ore trucks crossed the highway for a couple of years, causing several accidents and generally creating a traffic hazard, so the company tunneled under the road and reinforced over it; now the thundering ore-carriers pass beneath with no delay or risk of collision.

That day in late-March of 1967, we traversed several small creeks—very slowly to reduce risk of grounding the low-slung car—and after maneuvering around some small ice floes, found ourselves in the midst of a row of collapsed dark grey and rotting buildings, as well as the remains of what were once small false-fronted stores. We parked and got out and in no time Mary's eyes, now open wide, were the size of Victorian china saucers, which was good because that was the first thing she picked up.

"Five more and some cups and I can have a tea party," she exclaimed.

I picked through several garbage piles at the backs of buildings and found old bottles and beer cans and a small decorated bird house—then, almost completely buried, a large, twelve-inch-wide copper funnel, probably from a still or a brewing utensil. All went into my old backpack. We worked our way down *Main Street* and then Mary's eyes were drawn to a vivid blue-green turquoise glint near the threshold of a partially collapsed storefront. With her eye on it carefully, she almost tripped on the other end of a large object lying across the doorway. She caught herself on the door frame and looked down.

"It's a big piece of old tree trunk, probably infused with copper-green minerals," she called out, as she tried to lift it.

It was about five feet long, but it had large bulges at each end. I caught up with her and bent down to pick it up. But no, it was heavy and wet, and still frozen in. Did I say heavy? I finally pried one end out with an ugly six-foot piece of two-by-six with rusty nails protruding everywhere, and tried again. It moved, so Mary held up that end while I pried the other loose, then raised it slowly from its resting place.

They say there is nothing heavier in the world than the femur of a now-extinct woolly mammoth, and that's correct, for that's what it was—a full-size adult femur bone, former owner unknown, and hopefully not coming back to claim it.

Mary helped to lift it across my shoulders that I'd covered with an old burlap sack and I stumbled off toward our vehicle, almost dropping it twice on moss and ice as I slipped and lost my footing, sure that I was being followed by a rather annoyed three-legged mastodon.

Mary was ecstatic as we drove back. "There's one of these femurs on display in the university museum. Now I have my own."

The ribs are a good size here, but not a lot of meat on them.

I nursed a sore shoulder for a day or so.

The whole time, Ted Anderson was persistently asking, "Where did you take my car? It's filthy! And what was in the trunk?"

"Don't ask, it was a mammoth task!" I told him.

Later, I admired the great bone as it lay there, the new front step of Mary's cabin.

I lost track of *the bone* for a long time—well, fifty-two years to be exact, until the summer of 2019, when my wife Barbara went to Ketchikan for a statewide arts meeting. She along with others was invited later to go over to Mary Henrikson's house and studio to view her personal art collection…and there, yes right there, *in pride of place*, lying in repose on her reinforced mantelpiece was the massive femur of Mr. Mammoth himself, spending a well-earned retirement in a warm, dry place.

Bone idle, at last.

OFF TO KETCHIKAN,
SPRING 1967

When the UAF semester ended in early May, Mary was looking forward to seeing her mother and family in Ketchikan, so she left within a week, her departing words to me being, "I can probably get you a job at the cannery if you want one...I grew up there and my family knows lots of folks."

I had left Marine Science by this time, so within a couple more weeks I was all packed up, with two large suitcases carefully and safely stored in Pete and Nancy McRoy's cool, dry basement on Sprucewood Road in College.

I departed early one Friday morning on the Wien Airlines flight to Juneau via Whitehorse in the Yukon Territory. After a stopover in Juneau of a couple of hours, during which I transferred to the Coastal-Ellis Airlines dock in downtown Juneau, I boarded their PBY Catalina flying boat for Ketchikan via Petersburg and Wrangell. At that time, there were no airports at any of the towns on the rest of my journey. We took off from downtown Juneau by backing down on the wood timber ramp, then once afloat, the wheels were retracted and we taxied out and took off on the Gastineau Channel, steering around several fishing boats and a large Alaska ferry almost filling the channel headed to Sitka.

We flew straight down Stephen's Passage with tall mountains on both sides for about an hour and then into clouds and soon after, *kerflomp!* We landed in three-foot chop in Petersburg, the flying boat cavorting like a hooked king salmon, a standard event for everyone on the flight, it seemed, except me. The next hop was to Wrangell, just minutes away. The PBY flew low over tree tops and barely skirted several mountains. On arrival I looked out, sure I'd be seeing spruce tips and rocks caught in the landing gear. It was a similar flight to Ketchikan, low, scenic, and slightly alarming.

I gathered my luggage in the crowded terminal, turned around, and there was Mary with a hug and an enormous smile.

"Well, are you ready"

"For what?" I asked.

"To celebrate, have a drink."

"Why?"

"Well, I'm here, plus I've got you a job—you start at Ward Cove on Monday morning!" She laughed, her smile even bigger.

"What? Where? Who?" is all that came out of me.

We drove to her sister Nancy's house first and had a drink. Nancy was another Nordic blonde with blue eyes and pale complexion. Her husband, Jonathon Dewitt, was a well-respected Tlingit leader who later had bestowed on him the high honor of becoming Chief Shakes IX. Their two sons had dark hair and skin and pale blue eyes.

I didn't think about the job. After all, I had ten years of research lab experience in hand, so how hard could this job be at Cove's Ward—*must be part of the Ketchikan hospital*, I thought.

Then I heard Mary casually say to her sister, "Mom got Ron on at the cannery. He starts Monday and can stay in the bunkhouse."

"Cannery? Bunkhouse? What sort of lab is that?" I enquired.

Nancy chimed in with, "You'll be slave labor around the cannery for Mean Joe Brindle. If you're lucky, you'll survive all the grunt work and escape to a boat when the fishing starts…" her voice trailed off with no smile.

WARD COVE CANNERY, 1967

By the time my day started at eight on Monday morning, most of the cannery was bustling. I signed in at the office, where I was informed that I would be joining a union—the United Fishermen of Alaska—and it would be a forty-hour work week until fishing started and then *maybe you get on a boat* or you spent the summer creosoting the pilings underneath the Filipino bunkhouse or similar pleasant task!

Mean Joe Brindle was just as mean as Mary's sister described him. *When I say jump, you just say how high!* was one of his oft repeated yells. He was terse and bossy. Well, he was the boss, so I and everyone else jumped to it on his orders.

Part of my orientation that first day was to spend an hour or so in four different areas of the cannery, learning just what went on there. It started with Earl, a long-time employee at the cannery who ran the *retorts*, the giant steam ovens that looked like the engines of steam locomotives. Pallets containing hundreds of cans full of salmon would be wheeled on tracks into the retorts, which were then sealed and the steaming/sterilizing could begin.

The next area was the *Iron Chink*. This was a large machine that stood at the start of the fish processing line and removed the heads and tails of the fish. It also had an odd curved knife *cum* spatula that sliced open and scraped out most of the entrails, or as the *slime liners* called it, *the nuts, guts, and feathers*.

The Iron Chinks were made in Seattle by the Smith Machine Works and installed in canneries all over the Pacific Northwest and Alaska. Each machine had replaced several Chinese workers, hence the racist moniker bestowed on the device. Dave, the expert chink mechanic, had been at many canneries in Alaska and was now at Ward Cove. The one word that Dave carved into my brain that day, and even to this day makes my fingers search for my palms is: *never.*

"Never put your fingers anywhere in or near the chink when it's running or blocked."

He must have said that to me ten times that day.

"When the *slime chicks* shout, *It's stopped, but it's just a piece of fish head…look it's right there…just push it out with a finger,* no, never!"

The slime chicks were the girls who worked the processing line.

This machine replaced 10 Chinese laborers.

He pointed to a large electrical switch box on the floor. "Turn it off, then wait till the chink stops moving. Finally, grab a little strip of scrap wood from the pile there to clear the blockage."

The machine's name was cast into the top of the steel frame just as Dave's warning was etched into the top of my head.

My next step of *instant knowledge* was with Mike Amundsen, the general mechanic for the whole cannery. He told me that I would be helping *redo* the bathhouse in the Filipino bunkhouse. No envy attached to this task nor volunteers. It was a filthy, barely functioning large bathroom consisting of four stalls, no doors, broken urinals, and a couple of painted tin shower stalls with no curtains. The walls, however, were all finished off— i.e., covered in crude Spanish and *Tagalog* graffiti. We would be starting the redo of the Filipino bathroom once the large sheet metal urinal being made in town was brought out to the cannery—a brief reprieve.

It was quite normal, then as now, to have multiple nationalities working in Alaska towns and canneries in the summer and *walking the docks* looking for work. The slime chicks working on the processing line consisted of Native Alaskans, Nordic blondes, Filipinas, and a couple of brunettes from Seattle or even Bellingham. So, the presence of an itinerant Englishman meant little to nothing.

The fourth task was to be a general laborer. At eight a.m. every day, I would go straight to the large freight dock, which had several cranes mounted at the water's edge. I would find a broom and start sweeping, cleaning up in general. I would slide all the small items and any nails or screws—and there were many—straight into the water below through the large gaps between the dock timbers.

There were lots of odd people hanging around the cannery by that time of the summer—some old, some young, but all looking for a job.

One day, I was hard at it sweeping when a small figure wearing a brown derby and a gabardine overcoat stepped out of the shadows and rudely, I thought, accosted me.

"What do you think you're doing?"

Not knowing or really caring who it was, I barked back, "What do I think I'm doing? I don't *think* I'm doing anything, I *know* what I'm doing—cleaning up the dock area. Who are you, anyway?"

"I'm Wyn Brindle," he shot back.

"Oh, I work for Joe," I replied, dismissively.

"I'm his older brother. I own the cannery. And the National Bank of Alaska." He paused and gathered himself. "Do you know Dunn and Bradstreet?"

'I don't think so—are they the electricians?" I naively offered.

"They are an international credit rating corporation," he spat out, "and I am very wealthy and worth millions. And do you know how I got here?"

I didn't answer for a second, but thought, *well, I'm not wealthy and I'm about to become even less so!*

"No, I don't know," I replied softly.

He looked down at the pile of nails that were about to become part of the beach below, and said, shouting at me, "By saving items like that, so stop right there, get a cardboard box or something and pick up every nail and screw on this dock! Put the box in the workshop and the mechanics can reuse them."

"Ok, Wyn," I offered.

"And it's *Mr. Brindle* to you, boy!" was his final exhortation.

I increased my pace and swept the nails into piles that I picked up with a large dustpan. He watched me for a little while, then, after I'd picked up a particularly grand mound of metal, I looked up for approval, but he was gone. For the rest of the day, I waited for someone to call me to the office. At 5 p.m., hearing from no one, I slunk back to my room in the bunkhouse.

MOOSE DROPPING

The worst job I had was not, surprisingly, redoing the aforementioned Filipino bunkhouse toilet area, which was bad, but improved slightly because someone had gone in there the day before we started and washed down the entire area with a high-pressure fire hose. On the day that the toilet job started, I was warned by several people not to go down *there* without a baseball bat to defend myself. *They are all tied to street gangs in Seattle or the Phillipines* was the gist of several warnings I received. I ignored the *advice*, walked down with a small toolbox, and entered the room, only to be confronted by two large Filipino guys swaggering out, adjusting their pants.

"Ola," I said cautiously in my best north London schoolboy Spanish.

I followed with, "Que tal?"

Silence.

The smaller guy said, "Bueno, gracias, y usted?"

The larger, well-muscled one in cut-off jeans and a tank top added, "Tu es el Anglo, no? Y su hables espanol?"

"Si, pero, solo un poco," I replied, then added the line I would use later hundreds of times in Central and South America. "No hay Gringo aqui! Yo soy Ingles." Followed by, "Inglaterra, campiones del mundo."

"Bueno," they responded in unison, and we all smiled at each other as we shook hands and quickly started to talk what people all over have in common except Americans—football (soccer).

No, the worst job by far was *packing pipe* up the hillside opposite the cannery, replacing some of the pipeline that supplied water to the whole cannery from a mountain lake. The pipe was six inches in diameter, schedule 40, galvanized and came in about ten-foot lengths. It was extremely heavy. There was a crew of four of us assigned to move up and join it all together. We tied lines to each *joint* and then two of us dragged it up the hillside with one hand on the line and the other grabbing roots or rocks in order to maintain our balance and keep moving.

At various times during the day, Joe Brindle's moneybags brother would appear and berate us with, "Don't think you guys are going to make it onto a boat. You're all too slow."

That's not true, I thought.

"And you talk too much!" Which was definitely true.

Hauling the pipe was only half the job; we then had to carry forty-eight-inch pipe wrenches up the hill and join each piece to the next with couplings and pipe joint compound.

I never got to know the other guys really well, because at quitting time on about the fourth day of this *pipe dream*, Joe was waiting as we came down into the cannery. He called out the other guys' names one by one, following it with the name of a tender or a company-owned fishing boat.

When he got to me, he paused, then actually touched me on the shoulder and with a wry smile said, "You, will be deckhand on the *Sterling*. Get your gear stowed on board tonight. There'll be some work to do on the boat, but you'll leave soon."

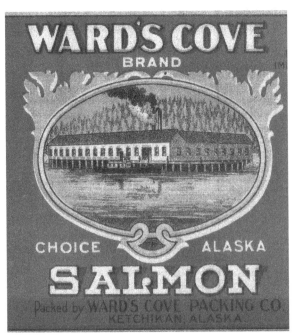

Ward Cove Salmon label with incorrect spelling (the apostrophe). Label courtesy of Karen Hofstad.

FRESH ON THE BOAT

The *Sterling* was one of the larger tenders that Ward Cove Cannery owned. She was a wooden ninety-foot former herring seiner, built in Washington State in the thirties. It now had a large Caterpillar diesel engine and was decked out in red and green with the hull and bulwarks painted black. She had a crew of four: Jake the captain, a fairly even-handed skipper, but a heavy consumer of alcohol when ashore; Dave the engineer, a young guy from Seattle who kept a very clean and organized engine room and helped me on deck as needed; Bill, a recovering alcoholic, the quiet but excellent cook; and me.

I retrieved my personal belongings from the bunkhouse that night and stowed them on a bunk in the *fo'c'sle* (forecastle), the bow area of a ship that usually houses the crew. The *Sterling* had a total of eight bunks, but two were always covered in tools of various kinds.

I spent some time on the deck of the boat examining how the lines were secured and where things were stowed. I left the vessel about eight-thirty and went to *mug up*, the traditional evening meal at a cannery which comprised leftovers from that day's lunches plus a delicious assortment of fresh-baked pies. I had gone to very few mug ups, since I usually met up with Mary and her friends, or we ate with her mother or her sister's family.

I slept well in the narrow bunk of the fo'c'sle and when fully awake climbed up on deck to a beautiful July sunlit morning. *Err...no*, this was Ketchikan, Alaska; it was cloudy and the rain was bucketing down in dark vertical shards that hit the deck, bounced up about two feet, then trickled down into your boots. We had rain like this in London, of course, and everyone said, *Man it's pissing down, but it won't last, it'll be over in an hour*, and it always was. But in Ketchikan, it could, and had, and did last for days on end. The average annual rainfall is 165 inches.

Jake, the skipper, put me at the helm after I'd cast off and watched me carefully as we headed down the channel into town and the fuel dock. We made way slowly in the obscure grayness as I steered around large blurred objects that became anchored vessels, and smaller ones that became channel markers, and always through driving rain. Jake moored the boat and I helped Bob the engineer fill the tanks with diesel fuel.

On the way back, Jake observed me again at the helm as I would be taking watches when others were asleep; he also began to explain the Loran C navigation system, which preceded GPS. It was a form of triangulation using very low frequency radio waves transmitted from a series of tall ground-based towers.

Jake took over the helm as we entered Ward Cove and there standing on the dock as we approached our mooring were Joe and Wyn Brindle, just idly chatting, but I thought, *this could be nail-biting*, remembering my time sweeping up on the dock under the mercenary gaze of Mr. Wyn.

I was on the bow and had the line ready, but neither of them moved or offered with a raised arm or anything to catch the line, so I caught sight of a small vertical mooring post with a crossarm in it about thirty feet ahead, and having made a large loop in the end, launched it in a curve ahead of the vessel. It sailed up into the driving rain, then out, and down and right over the bollard, and rested just long enough for me to pull the slack out of the line and secure it with a couple of turns to the deck cleats. I glance over at Joe and Wyn, not talking now, just staring at each other. No I didn't say, *nailed it*, but thought about it.

In the next few days, we stayed out and received the catch from several Ward Cove vessels, but the crews all agreed there were not a lot of fish. We delivered our load to the cannery and headed back out to wait for more calls. On the way to our anchorage south of Camano Point, the boat slowed way down and Jake called us all into the wheelhouse. *Uh oh,* I thought, *what's up now?*

He'd already turned the engine, the deck music, and the ship radio off, and we were almost stationary as we came alongside a large dark object in the water. It was a sleeping whale, a humpback at least fifty feet long. Jake said he'd seen this whale behavior before.

We remained right next to the enormous creature and watched, mesmerized in silence, as the leviathan just lay there on the surface. The story was that whales *turned off* half of their brain and kept an eye open with the other, hence the origin of the expression, *sleeping with one eye open.* The scientific truth that I heard recently from Dr Suzie Teerlink, a federal marine biologist in Juneau, is that they rest and recover with their entire brain in a very shallow state of sleep.

After a couple of minutes, the enormous eyelid nearest us slowly opened and the dark eye behind it observed us carefully, then with the slightest movement of its enormous black tail flukes, it slowly moved ahead of us and sank supremely beneath the surface. *Well, you don't see that on the Welsh Harp* (a popular park and reservoir in North London), I thought, as I gazed, both eyes wide open in wonder, at the sight before me.

We anchored in a quiet cove for the night, and with the soft lapping of waves on the hull next to my bunk I fell asleep. At about two a.m., I awoke to the boat moving at anchor in some wind, but just turned over in the bunk.

THE FISHING VESSEL *OREGONIAN*

The next sound I heard were those words from the ships radio dreaded by every person at sea: *Mayday, Mayday!* This simple English word is derived, of course, from the French phrase, *m'aidez*, meaning *help me*. I felt I was dreaming.

But then Jake yelled down into the f'o'csle, "Up you guys, now! Pull the hook, we're off."

The engine roared to life, we all stumbled around pulling our clothes on, plus raingear, and soon the vessel was moving.

"It's a fishing boat, a seiner, and according to the Mayday call is named the *Oregonian*. They claim they're sinking, but I honestly doubt it ." He smiled. "These calls happen now and again, usually someone overreacting. They fix the problem, pump the bilges, and that's the end of it."

We all nodded, but started to carefully scan the dawn light on the horizon. I did not know what, or really how, to do anything in an emergency like this could be shaping up to be. Were there other boats? Where was the Coast Guard? Rescue helicopters?

We relaxed a little and grabbed coffee, then as I returned to the bridge three words blared from the radio: *Sinking! Sinking! Abandon....* And then, nothing, nothing at all.

Jake got on the horn and with the mic shaking along with his voice, gave the Coast Guard in Juneau our position: we were about ten miles south of Camano Point. He also told Dave the engineer to go below and check the engine room, as he pushed the speed control up to the max.

We were in a serious hurry now, the boat pushing through four-foot waves and rolling a little. The wind increased, as did the waves. The cook made up a pan of scrambled eggs and ham, which we took in turns to gulp straight from the stove. Back in the wheelhouse, Jake told Dave to ready some longer lines near the stern.

He turned to me. "Ron, get up on the bow and sort out several longer lines out of the deck box. Keep them ready to throw to survivors."

I gulped. This was getting real and in a hurry.

"There! She's gone!" shouted Jake a few minutes later. Coming into sight floating toward us in the waves were a number of unsecured items from the deck of the now disappeared vessel. Lines, plastic bottles, brooms, some with and some without handles, coolers, then the large deck box floated past, rocking jauntily in the swells.

I was coiling the lines on the port bow when Jake leaned out of the wheelhouse and yelled, "I'll keep heading into the wind like we're going. I'll be able to control the speed of the boat so we don't run over anyone in the water. It'll make it harder for you to throw into the wind—you'll just have to do it!"

I was speechless and just nodded as I zipped up my rain jacket to my chin and pulled my wool watch cap down more firmly. More flotsam and jetsam went by, including part of the seine net from the stern of the *Oregonian*.

Then, just behind a large plastic Clorox bottle and in front of a piece of pressure-treated four-by-four, my eyes fixed on two arms flailing away either side of a human head with an open mouth.

Jake screamed, "Throw it! Now!"

I grasped the coiled line with one hand, reared back, and threw with all my might.

The line missed the pleading arms by at least six feet. I dropped the line to the deck and grabbed the other one with both hands, ignoring Jake's crude language cursing my birthright and my homeland. This time I braced my waist against the stout rail and looked for the arms…they were…gone. No…oh…no! But wait, here they are again, yes, just briefly covered by waves. I reared back and summoned all my (cricket, rugby, and soccer) strength to move to my arms and shoulders, and let it fly….

I did not see its path because I was struggling to regain my balance as I hung over the rail, staring into the waves below. I heard that it soared up and out and the crew swore later that the wind subsided at that very moment for a second or so. Thank you Aeolus!

Well, it hit him on the head, *smack!* One arm came up, grabbed the line, then the other. I ran down the rail, dodging the cleats, to the working deck area, hauling in the lifeline as I went. Dave nodded, smiling and said, "It's a keeper," as he threw a backup line to our *catch* in the water.

The survivor held on to both lines and as he came up to the hull we both reached over, grabbing hold of lines, clothing, anything, and hauled him almost straight up, and driven by adrenaline, over the gunwale. We held him steady as the cook wrapped a blanket around him and helped him shuffle into the warmth of the galley.

Jake's voice interrupted any sense we might have had of accomplishment. "Come on goddamn it. Look, out there, there's two more. One of them appears out of it!"

I ran to the bow, coiling my line as I went, and quickly spotted the guy that looked *out of it*. I threw my double-handed, waist-on-rail, *patented launch*. It landed right next to him in the water with a splash. His head rolled up and back as he opened his eyes and grabbed the rope. I waited a second or two, closed my gaping mouth, and then started hauling him in. Dave, down near the stern, threw a long line to the third guy, who was actually swimming a bit amidst piles of trash.

We rescued three people on that day, employing the adrenaline strength that is sometimes granted to ordinary beings to perform extraordinary tasks in moments of imminent danger.

The *Sterling* then began a series of transits, back and forth, plotted on a map grid. We had saved three souls, but there were five on the vessel. We stayed in the area of the sinking for about two hours, but we had to get the survivors to town. There were no survival suits with radio beacons in those days, so we were soon relieved by two fishing boats, and left the area headed for the dock in Ketchikan. Above us we heard the *wop, wop, wop* of a helicopter, but didn't see a thing in the lowering skies, driving rain, and wind—Aeolus was back. The owner of the boat and a crewmate were never found.

We all sat squeezed into the humid warmth of the galley. I looked across at the soaking wet bodies wrapped in blankets. They were all three wiping their eyes or sobbing. One of them was the son of the boat's owner, another a part owner of the Ketchikan Spruce Mills, and the other a local Ketchikan resident.

An ambulance at the city dock picked up the three survivors and took them to the hospital. The *Sterling* arrived back at the Ward Cove Cannery an hour or so later. Mary was waiting on the dock and as I greeted and held her, she shook with fear and relief. We went back to the bunkhouse, shared some beers, and fell asleep amid the pleasures of being alive.

The southeast salmon season ended abruptly a few days later, becoming the worst season in history, before or since. I worked around the cannery for a week or so, closing up different areas. I was called to the office one morning and handed my payoff check. Things were somber in there, but as

I examined my check, Joe Brindle appeared, shook my hand, and thanked me—no hugs in those days. I never saw him again, but understand the family all moved years later to Lake Union, Washington, where their property holdings made them all millionaires. I know, I checked their Dunn and Bradstreet!

Mary and I met almost every night, grabbed a bite to eat, and then went barhopping. *There's the Limey that helped save the three souls off the* Oregonian, was a usual refrain, although sometimes not so polite. For a while, I actually got more attention than Mary (well, maybe!). What I do know is that in every bar and restaurant in Ketchikan, and there are a lot, we never paid for a drink for the rest of our time there that summer.

OREGONIAN (1967)   The 49 foot wood seiner *Oregonian* sank near Caamano Point northwest of Ketchikan Tuesday, August 8, 1967. Rudolph (66) Johanson, known as "Joe" was lost. His son, Rudy Johanson, skipper of the *Oregonian*, Ed Borgan, Erne Johnson and David Phillips were rescued. The Johansons had purchased the vessel two years before as a burned out hull and rebuilt it at the Salmon Bay Fishermen's Terminal.

Mapping and Location: Southeast Alaska   55 30 N 131 58 W   Chart 17420

Additional Information: Tonnage 45 Gross 30 Net, Length 49.2, Breadth 15.5, Depth 7.1, Built 1918 Tacoma WA, ON 216109, Call Sign WA8946

Sources: 1. *Merchant Vessels of the U S* (1965) Pg 522, **2.** *Bellingham Herald* (August 9, 1967) "Search Underway for Fishermen" Pg 1, **3.** *Seattle Daily Times* (October 11, 1967) "Rudolph Johanson" Obit Pg 89

From *The Alaska Shipwrecks, 1750-2015,* by Captain Warren Good and Michael Burwell, author and marine tragedy expert.

Back to Fairbanks
via Seattle

Mary's family had a vehicle that needed to be taken to Seattle. I think it belonged to a sister of hers, so we agreed to take it south via the ferry to Prince Rupert, British Columbia.

As we readied the car, Mary's sister Nancy casually said to me, "It's raining, you know, in Fairbanks!"

"Not unusual," I replied. "Fairbanks gets all its rain, and only ten or twelve inches at that, in the summer."

I didn't pay any attention to her remark until we got on the ferry about a week later and a crewmember, on hearing that I lived in Fairbanks said, *Boy, it's been raining there, hasn't it?* The ferry trip was quite pleasant—no rain at all. We disembarked at Rupert and headed out for Prince George—it's a full day's drive, five hundred miles or so of soaring peaks, glacial valleys, and fast-flowing rivers.

It's a distance to Seattle, so another two days passed before we drove south through Bellingham. I asked Mary where her sister lived.

She kind of gritted her teeth and said, "Broadmoor."

I was silent; my insides gripped with the horror of the word. *Broadmoor* in England, as every British schoolboy knows, is a major psychiatric prison about an hour southwest of

London. On a hundred fenced acres, it's technically a *hospital for the criminally insane*, a dark, brooding Victorian brick pile with a large gated entrance sporting a clock tower—*Your time starts/ends here*, depending on which way you're going.

When I had finished explaining all this to Mary, I cautiously inquired as to what her sister's Broadmoor was like.

"Oh it's gated all right, and fenced too."

I asked her what her sister had done to be in there.

"Oh, she married a lawyer."

After showing our IDs, the security man at the gate almost saluted as he waved us through. We entered a universe of manicured lawns, with all animals, including cats, on leashes, and immaculately kept houses, if not mansions. We spent a couple of nights with Mary's sister and her husband, then went downtown and rented a room at *Seattle's Alaskan hotel*—The Stewart, close by the Pike Place market on Stewart Street, and now a parking lot.

On checking in, the talk was all about the rain in Fairbanks. *She's bankfull, and about to flood*, was the oft-heard remark in the small lounge area, referring to the Chena River that flows down from the surrounding hills, and meanders through downtown Fairbanks.

We spent time in the downtown area, and also checked out the U-District, with its varied nightlife on University Avenue. I even ran into an acquaintance from Fairbanks, who started to talk about…yes, you've got it—the rain!

I was now thinking that I'd better return fairly soon and Mary also felt she should be returning to college, which she'd earlier decided was going to be Central Washington State in Ellensburg. A couple of days later, we said good-bye and I took the shuttle bus from the hotel to SeaTac airport.

I bought a standby ticket to Fairbanks. *It's flooded, and bad*, said the young assistant at the Alaska Airlines counter. The plane was full and all the talk on board was about the *high humidity* in town, and *got your break-up boots?*

THE GREAT FLOOD

The great flood of 1967 began with heavy rainfall for weeks in the surrounding hills of a town that then only held about 18,000 people. Between the 8th and 15th of August, the Chena River, usually a placid tributary of the much larger Tanana River, overflowed its banks with more than thirty times its carrying capacity and rose more than fifteen feet at the Cushman Street bridge.

The extent of the 1967 flood: Chena River in blue, Foodland Supermarket marked with an X, and Creamers Field is the white area near top.

SHORT'S STORIES

The entire town and surrounding areas were inundated in three to four feet of water, plenty for boats of all types to utilize. Several rescues were made, some of people, but many more, as we heard, of tents, sleeping bags, and other outdoor equipment from Pinska's Store on Cushman Street, Carr's Clothing, and many other businesses. Canoes were seen being paddled rapidly along on a one-way rescue, still with their price tags attached!

As the waters receded, a one-inch layer of glacial silt, soft beige mud deposited by the river, lay on every horizontal surface. It was also inside many half-empty alcohol bottles, as every bar and restaurant owner soon discovered.

Top: Army truck on Lacey Street as a riverboat crosses on 4th Avenue... *but did they stop at the light?* Bottom: After the flood, 6000 Fairbanksans stayed at the university on the hill. Here some of them are lining up for food. I'm in the back somewhere.

Arrived without
Break-up Boots

It seemed that in those days we always got a ride from the airport to the U, usually arranged in the luggage area. It was less than three miles. We made it across University Avenue Bridge, but the water was lapping at the sidewalks as we reached the intersection with College Road. There, our eyes were flooded with a dozen river boats of various kinds still tied up at the base of the hill. Our ride, quickly garnered with other students, sloshed through the large intersection and climbed the hill to the main campus.

The campus was high and dry, but there were people everywhere. They had opened all the dorms to folks who had been flooded out because the semester did not begin for several weeks. There were about seven thousand dislocated persons who were now occupying every nook and cranny on the campus.

A few days after my arrival, my main task was to go back down to *Waterworld*, or to be more exact, to Pete and Nancy McRoy's pleasant log house on Sprucewood Road and collect my belongings that I'd stored in their warm and bone-dry basement before leaving for Ketchikan. Their house was off Geist Road and about equidistant between the campus and the Chena River. I got a ride down with someone going back to the airport. There was water everywhere, and mud, and people already bringing out couches and other odorous household goods to dry out on high spots on lawns and yards. When I arrived at the McRoy's house, I was surprised to find my belongings already outside on the front steps, right next to… more mud.

"I'm afraid it started to smell, so I had to get it out of the basement," Nancy said as she smiled. "We've already taken a couple of loads of our silt-laden, mildewy stuff to the dump."

She was going back up to campus—*dry world*, as she called it—to her job as a linguist, so I got a ride back to Hess Hall. There, I opened and sorted my clothes outside in the parking lot. A lot of it went straight into the dumpster next to the back door of the building, the rest straight into the hall washing machines.

I had pre-registered at Hess Hall, a dormitory for "mature" students, and had already moved my luggage from Seattle into a temporary room. After a few days, permanent space was assigned to me upstairs.

I had unpacked a lot and was attempting to slide my suitcase under the bed when it kept hitting what seemed like heavy metal and wood objects. I pulled my suitcase back and also dragged out several rifles and shotguns when the door opened and in walked a guy who seriously demanded of me, "What are you doing with my firearms?"

"Yours? " I shot back. "They're under my bed. They're mine!"

We fired off several verbal volleys at each other, and then relaxed a bit, shook hands, and introduced ourselves.

"I'm a strong supporter of the second amendment," he went on to say.

"Yeah, I have guns too, but not in my bedroom. That's where bad accidents happen," I countered.

We eventually became friends in that dorm room and have remained so to this day. He was, and still is, Bob Bauman, and like me lives primarily in Fairbanks. We chatted with each other recently in a bookstore in town at the beginning of the Covid 19 pandemic. I almost always open the conversation with, *Hello Bob, I'm coming for your guns*, and grinning, he replies, *I'm ready for you Ron, and oh, how's your wife and family?*

He's just as *prepped* now as then, with a large arsenal of firearms and a large extended family to protect. This time he added, with a wink, "I have more guns now in order to protect my large stash of toilet paper!"

We shared the small (but loaded!) room for a couple of months, then I moved across the hall to a much larger one with a lapsed Catholic Zen laborer, and disc jockey, named John Ave-Lallemant. John had a janitor job at the Murphy Dome Air Force Station and also a position at the campus radio station, KUAC-FM, where he took *board shifts*, presented PSAs, played classical music, and read articles that came over the ticker tape.

He received several phone calls late one night on the hall phone and announced to me the next day that he had a family emergency *back east*. He would have to leave for about two weeks and asked if I would cover the news part of his shift while he was away.

"The other guys will cover the rest," he said. "Come up to the station later and I'll show you how to work the board."

THE RON SHORT REPORT

Later that day, I climbed the stairs and entered the station offices. The radio station in those days was on the top floor of Constitution Hall, which also housed the student union offices and café—the SUB.

Immediately, a guy with graying hair and beard, looking dapper and slightly familiar, stood up with outstretched hand and said, "Hi—Kenny Rogers."

"Oh. Hi," I said. "Ronan Short. Are you the station manager?"

"No. Are you?" was his quizzical response.

Luckily this was soon ended when the actual manager, Charlie Northrip, I believe, entered and directed me across the hall to the control room. Kenny Rogers and the First Edition were on their first tour out of California, so he was waiting in the office to do a pre-show interview for the radio station.

John Ave explained to me the basic functions of the KUAC control board and had me practice. He also showed me the teletype machine, which brought in all news and sports from the Associated Press (AP) wire.

"We're supposed to read each story and edit as needed for clarity, but usually there's no time, so it's just *rip and read.*"

I had read a couple of local announcements when a tap on my shoulder caused me to turn, and there was Kenny Rogers himself. I killed the mic quickly, which I'd just learned how to do.

"What's the name of your show?" he said with a grin.

Without another thought I said, "The Ron Short Report."

He gestured for me to turn on the mic and in his deep, resonant tone announced, "Please support KUAC and this— The Ron Short Report."

I was highly amused as he smiled, waved, and left the control room.

I got some *feedback* from this, but not as much as when a few evenings later I started to fulfill every British schoolboy's dream of reading live and slowly on the radio the English football (soccer) results. These were always intoned slowly and methodically. As a child I never really understood why, but as I grew older I realized almost every adult in the room was listening carefully and marking each result or *draw* (tie game) on a sheet of paper: *Doing the Pools*. This was the only method of off-track betting allowed at the time and was rigorously controlled by the government via two or three firms. The prize usually awarded each week was the equivalent and massive sum then of about US$200,000. The prizes were all paid in full, with all taxes paid by the pools companies. To win was considered a life-changing event.

I got such a kick out of reading the results the first time that I repeated the same lists about three times a week. The big surprise was that several British, Australian, and Irish residents of the Fairbanks area called up during the first week and demanded, with tongue in cheek, to know who I was, and *what the hell does he think he's doing?* followed by, *I've always wanted to do that!*

I met several UAF faculty and other residents with British connections during that time and have remained good friends with many to this day.

THE VERY STRANGE VEHICLE
PARKED OUTSIDE THE SUB

I had been back from Ketchikan for a while when one morning as I was settled in on the third floor of Hess Hall, a voice from the hallway accosted me.

"Hey Ron, is that your rig out there with all the gas cans and stuff tied on the front and back?"

"What are you talking about? No, I'd never own anything like that."

"Well, it's got your flag *writ large* on the front, too," said my amused dorm buddy, George Ziegler.

I ran to the nearest window and stared over at a vehicle parked right at the SUB steps. It was a 1950s-era British Land Rover all right, with an English license plate; an extra-large extended front bumper cradled four military-style five-gallon gas cans and the front of a large tool box mounted to a steel roof rack was painted with a large Union Jack flag. At the rear were still more fuel cans slung underneath, near the bumper.

The oddity continued after I'd run down the stairs and over to it, where I read the sign that was affixed to both sides of the vehicle. It read in large letters: *TRANS-CONTINENT AGRICULTURE EXPEDITION*.

I was amused as much as I was baffled, so I quickly ran into the SUB and after looking around for about a second, *spotted the culprits*, as they say.

Throw it down and keep a lookout for lions, and I don't mean the tea shop.

A Jeremy Ainsworth and a Michael (aka Mik) Crawford were both sipping coffees as we introduced ourselves. We became acquainted then and there, and good friends soon after. They had titled their venture after studying agriculture together at college in England and desiring to know more about it in other parts of the world. They got funding from a small British oil company—Duckhams—and compiled a record of their travels entitled, *Three Men's Meat*.

By the time they reached Fairbanks right after the flood in 1967, they had traversed the world learning about agriculture (and each other) for several years. They'd started out from England with a third college student—a Londoner by the name of Roger Smith, who left the group in Australia and hurried back to the UK to catch up with his new fiancée. According to Jeremy, he rode back the entire way from Singapore on an old Indian motorcycle.

Jeremy and Mik were able to help many people stuck in their homes or wading in the streets after the flood. Their Land Rover, for its round-the-world trip, had a special raised exhaust system that enabled the vehicle to traverse water up to five feet deep. As the waters subsided, Jeremy got work in Fairbanks helping a local plumbing company and Mik did the same, expediting for a construction outfit.

They left Alaska in October of '67, drove down the Alcan Highway, then across Canada and down to New York, from where they shipped the Land Rover, and then flew home to the UK.

The following year, I would travel with Mik the length of Central America and on to Colombia. Unfortunately, I lost contact with Mik many years ago, but Jeremy and I are still good friends. He is, and has been for many years, into aviation, flying all over Alaska and the Pacific, while dealing in Maule aerobatic (STOL) airplanes. Nowadays, he also has a small bulldozer and supports fire-fighting operations in Northern California!

Always getting ready. Roger Smith, Mik Crawford, and Jeremy Ainsworth.

PSST! WANNA GET SOME?

In 1967, and for several years after, the university was not in Fairbanks, technically, but in College, Alaska, an unincorporated *nonentity* located at the bottom of *Hippie Hill*. College consisted of several churches and a couple of small grocery stores, including the well-known Lindy's and the College Inn, but no alcohol sales whatsoever were allowed.

The nearest place to buy any alcohol was two miles away in a building that resembled a European nightmare with a matching linguistic contortion as its name—*The Switzerland*. It was owned and run by a certain Max Fueg, a volatile and quite racist citizen of the aforementioned country, who favored resolving any disputes by appearing out of the kitchen brandishing a very large knife. The only other establishment that sold alcohol then was the B & M Market, an early convenience store a couple of miles down College Road in Lemeta.

However, in the fall of '67 after the flood, the entire town was awash—in booze!

The Alcohol Beverage Control Board (ABC) had, after the flood waters subsided, condemned all sales from previously opened bottles of liquor of any kind, and even mentioned silt-covered, sealed bottles, with or without labels.

My first experience with the new *market* was while I was standing outside the College Inn one day. A shaggy-haired, bearded older man said, "*Psst*—I've got half a bottle of peppermint schnapps, a quarter bottle of Orange Curacao, and an almost full bottle of a tan-colored liquid. Interested?"

I quickly demurred and left the area thinking, *what was all that about?* and *what would I mix those with?*

It soon became a common event—partially empty bottles of liquor were for sale everywhere. They were supposed to have been destroyed at the landfill under the watchful eye of an ABC official. Some were, but most never made it halfway down Cushman Street before being diverted to houses, cabins, and apartments.

Some *sales* even occurred in bars. I was in the Nevada Bar on First Avenue one afternoon when a guy leaned over to me. "Hey buddy, almost a half bottle of Amaretto, with a dash of Chena water. Five bucks?"

"No thanks."

That might have been an early sighting of the later well-known schmoozer and raconteur, F. Bruce Haldeman. Whisky was sometimes found in full bottles, but opened and with no label—it was usually a mixture of Johnnie Walker and Bushmills, known as *Scotch-Irish*. It sold for five to seven bucks.

It's a good thing that Baileys Irish Cream did not exist then. The same color and consistency of the Chena River, it would never have sold after the flood.

One night not long after, I drove down to Tommy's Elbow Room in my old VW bug, hoping to acquire—either outside or in—a bottle of *flood booze*, as it was sometimes called. Not much going on outside, I ventured in, got a beer, and glanced around at the crowded seating area. There, sitting at a table, were two attractive young co-eds from Wickersham Residence Hall, Gayla Jacobs and Gwen Juster, dressed for a night out.

"You going to the party?" said Gayla, whom I'd met on campus.

"What party"?

"There's a bash in Lemeta, sort of a bootleg booze thing," said Gwen. "Do you have wheels?"

"Yes, and they go round and round," clarifying that my car was not *off the road* at that time. We finished our drinks and piled into the bug.

The party was at an apartment right off College Road and we followed the music right to the door, which was open as I remember. As the three of us strolled in, I caught sight of a tall guy I'd seen on campus. However, he'd already seen me and was moving across the living room floor with a *little haste.*

"Yeah, I've seen you around the SUB. You're one of those foreign students, you hang out on Chena Ridge, and smoke dope! We don't want any dope smokers here, so you gotta leave now—but the chicks can stay."

I was about to contest his description of me, but realized it was basically all true, so all I gave was my name followed by, "Who are you?"

"Doug Pope," came his reply, "and I'm from Badger Road. Come girls, let's get a drink. We have a lot of *flood bottles* here to choose from." He grabbed Gayla's arm and started over to the overflowing bottle collection on the sideboard.

"Er— No. I don't think so," she quickly replied, unlinking his arm...although gazing awhile at the number of half-filled bottles with few labels.

Gwen had by now firmly grasped my other arm. "The three of us are together so we can all stay or all leave."

"That British guy's not staying, he's a troublemaker—so there," said Doug. He slightly clenched his fists and started to inch toward me.

Gayla had by now grabbed my other arm and quickly offered, "Hey, make peace not war. We're all leaving...bye!"

As I turned, I think I said something like, "My arms are for loving not fighting!" I hope it was that good.

Outside, Gwen reached into one of her parka pockets and produced a familiar-looking half-filled bottle of whisky with only a tiny fraction of a label remaining on it.

"It was on the kitchen table on the way out. I'm sure it's Crown Royal. They'll never miss it with what's in there."

We went back to my room in Hess Hall and greatly enjoyed the *foreign* whisky that would soon *flood* the streets of Fairbanks.

Doug Pope and I have been firm friends now for close on fifty years. Following his time as a Lemeta party bouncer, he had a long career as a successful defense attorney in Anchorage. We both maintain houses in Alaska and vacation homes in Washington State and our families are in regular contact.

Gayla Jacobs later married falconer and artist Bill Tilton and Gwen Juster was recently heard from living with her partner in Anchorage. Cheers to you all!

A FREE TRIP TO ANCHORAGE

Later in the fall of 1967, I received a letter in the mail from the United States Government. A tax refund, I assumed, and gleefully tore it open looking for the check, only to find it was from the Selective Service Board (SSB). The rather ominous first word in it was, *Greetings*.

I was duly ordered to appear at the Board's offices in Anchorage for a medical exam in preparation for being drafted into the US Army. I had a green card, but was not a citizen.

This was close to the height of the Vietnam War, which I was opposed to, and young men were being drafted by the thousands, given basic training, and shipped overseas to *Nam*. I was not a pacifist, but did not agree with all the political maneuverings that got us into the conflict.

I called the phone number, duly registered, and a few days later a travel warrant arrived in the mail. I presented it at the airport a week later and was soon at the second story offices of the SSB medical board in downtown Anchorage. The room was very long, almost windowless, and decorated in three shades of grey paint. It was uncomfortably appointed with long wooden benches and a few hard metal chairs.

In the first area, a young freckled-faced non-commissioned officer ordered us all to, "Strip to the waist and stand at attention."

"Jesus," I said, "you'd think we're in the bloody army."

"We will be soon," nervously remarked a young native man, whose name turned out to be Silas, standing next to me as we both glanced around filled with apprehension.

I had pondered this scenario earlier and had asked around the U of A campus before I left. I learned that if you passed the physical, there was usually a brief window of a few weeks before you were actually drafted and ordered to report to a military base for basic training. This was when you could leave the country and not be branded a *draft dodger.*

So my plan was to do just that...take the Pan Am flight leg from Fairbanks to Tokyo, continue on to Hong Kong and down through Southeast Asia to Australia to see my cousin Anne and her family as planned years ago, then perhaps even back to England.

The next screened-off area was similarly decorated, and intentionally uncomfortable. The next order came. "Now take off all of your remaining clothes and place them on the floor. Do not stand up, but reach back, grasp your buttocks and *spread-em!*"

Many of the assembled were now in a mild state of shock, but all I could think of was the finale of several rugby songs where a similar move occurred and the "brown eye" was presented to all...and laughter and cheers followed.

Nothing like that here. An officer and an NCO bent down and peered into each rectum as words were mumbled. I also heard at least one rectum mumble. Clipboards were shuffled and notes taken.

We were then all seated on a long bench and an officer moved down the line on a typist's chair on wheels. When he got to me, he felt my torso then, working down to my lower legs, he ran his fingers over my shins.

He suddenly stopped. He looked up with a look of shock. "How did you get injured like this, and both legs, too?"

"I've never been injured."

"Looks like you've broken both your shins in the past, in several places," he went on, and began to shake his head.

"I've played soccer all my life, and rugby too in the last few years. I'm fine".

"Can you run long distances?" he asked, with more head shaking.

I began to see the light at the end of the examination.

"I can run a little," I lied, "but I couldn't run for a bus, or anything like that."

I was now thinking, *could this be possible…?*

The officer stood up and gravely intoned, "Son, you are not eligible for the United States Army."

I breathed deeply, but surreptitiously.

I realized I was pushing my luck, but still added, "Really? I could join the British Army tomorrow."

The medical officer now puffed out his chest a little. "Maybe so, but you are not eligible for the US Army."

I was then ordered to pick up my clothes and get dressed. I was handed some papers and shown the door.

On the stairs out, I ran into the young native Alaskan. He was all smiles. "I flunked. I had rickets and I'm very bowlegged. You?"

"Yes, broken bones in my legs."

We both laughed and walked straight across the street into a bar where we both toasted each other—*To defective human beings, Ronan and Silas.*

On the flight back to Fairbanks, I penned the following piece of simple verse, which I still remember—

Your Uncle Sam he called me down
To see if I was man
Enough to go and fight his rotten war in Vietnam.
He looked in every orifice, then into my eye
Alien—he said, get dressed—you're classified 1Y.

A FLICKER OF CREATIVITY

The Student Union Building on the University of Alaska, Fairbanks campus was and still is officially called Constitution Hall. This was where the delegates met in 1955-56 to create and flesh out the Alaska Constitution—a progressive and respected document. The founders studied all other state constitutions for guidance on what and what not to co-opt. It was ratified on April 4, 1956 and included, unique for its time, articles on civil rights and natural resources. I later met a number of the founders, including Ralph Rivers, Frank Peratrovich (the only Native Alaskan), and Katie Hurley, one of only six women among the forty-nine writers.

By 1967, the SUB had become the social center of the campus, with a snack bar and many tables that drew student meetings. It was altogether pleasant except for the original garish neon lighting and greenish décor that greeted those delegates in 1955.

So it wasn't the surroundings that stimulated most of us, but the company. The particular group that I became attached to was a section of the English department faculty known as *the flying poets*. They consisted of Edmund Skellings, Robert King, Larry Wyatt, Kenneth Warfel, and Donald Kaufmann, all published writers in their fields and well-known around campus. Once or twice a year, they would charter a plane and fly to smaller communities in Alaska, reciting their own poems and prose works and encouraging young students in *the bush* to create their own.

The campus at this time was still buzzing from the visit some months earlier by the famous writer Norman Mailer. He had delivered several lectures and participated in a couple of the Alaska Writers Workshops. According to my long-time friend Joyce Hughes Rivers, all these events were packed houses with loud raucous readings and interruptions culminating at least once in a bar fight in the International Hotel and Bar, aka the Big I.

So it was at one of the daily lunch meetings, with a couple of the SUB tables pushed together that, with apprehension, I offered my brief one-liner to Ed Skellings, a senior English professor and a Ph.D. graduate of the esteemed Iowa Writers Workshop.

"Here Ed," I mumbled, "I've written something."

He turned slowly and without a word took the piece of paper out of my hand and began to study it.

"I like it," he said. "but let me guide you a little about pauses in poems. We call them caesuras, and here you need a big one. Plus," he added smiling, "I've just doubled your entire volume of poetry—now you have two lines!"

My first poetic effort made it through several workshops and was eventually included in my thesis as part of my MFA.

The Florist
He made artificial flowers so real
They died.

FROM COLD TO WET TO HOT

I was taking a couple of science courses that fall of 1967, but was more interested in the writing classes and hanging around with Ed Skellings and others, all of us jotting down ideas that were guided by the Alaska Writers Workshop.

As the semester came to an end in December, I received a phone call on the dormitory phone in Hess Hall. It was my sister Sally. She had by then been in Hawaii for about eighteen months—the same time I had resided in Alaska. She had secured a good job as a marine technician at the University of Hawaii's ocean science lab at Coconut Island at the edge of Kaneohe Bay on the island of Oahu. She said that she had a very small apartment in Waikiki, but I could stay there with her, and we could travel around and see *the islands* over the Christmas holidays.

I jumped at the idea, as it was then about twenty-five below zero. I planned on getting a standby ticket first to Seattle then on to Honolulu—the standard manner by which we all traveled in those days. I retained my room with John Ave-Lallemant at the Hess Hall dorm for the next semester and a few days later was half asleep in the back row of an Alaska Airlines red-eye flight droning off to Seattle.

SeaTac Airport then was much smaller than now, and soon after deplaning I was standing outside delighting in the feel of soft rain on my face and a slight breeze in the air. It was, of course, forty degrees *above* zero and everything was wet, a big change for me then, as it still is when leaving Alaska in the winter. As I like to say nowadays, the temperature is the same—forty degrees; it's just that there is a minus sign in front of the four in Fairbanks!

I had to wait a couple of hours for my next flight, which if memory serves was on United Airlines. It was another standby flight, and I ate, drank, and then dozed across three seats close to the back of the plane.

When the doors of the plane opened in Honolulu, a gush of warm tropical air enveloped us all as we deplaned. The next thing I knew, a young Hawaiian woman in a floral skirt and a skimpy top stepped up close as if she knew me, planted a kiss on my cheek saying *Aloha, welcome to Hawaii*, and placed a *lei* around my neck.

Well, hello, I said, hoping to linger with her, but she was gone and already about four passengers away down the line, completing the gracious and time-honored Hawaiian ritual of arrival.

The entire airport—all concourses and walkways—was open to the elements and suffused with the aromas of tropical plants and flowers. I collected my checked luggage, strode outside into the heat, and then, as Sally had instructed me, looked for a local bus with *Waikiki* on the front. I thought back to our last telephone call....

"Get off at Queen Liliuokalani Street," she said.

"What? Where?" I mumbled.

"It's Hawaiian. She was the last Queen of Hawaii. The language is interesting; you'll learn it. And, oh yes, I'll be there waiting for you."

The bus came in a few minutes. I cradled my small suitcase on my lap and observed the scenery and the passengers: a few tourists, but mainly bored locals going to work in the giant Ala Moana Center or nearby hotels.

I got off at *Queen whatsit* Street and Sally was there looking radiant with long blonde hair and a big smile for her *big bruvver.*

"You look so pale," she laughed, as she hugged and kissed me hello.

We crossed busy Kalakaua Avenue as she explained that all of the big hotels blocked the sight of the entire waterfront, but there was a right-of-way through any and all of them to the beach.

Her apartment was only a couple of blocks away—and was not small. No, it was tiny. She had borrowed a nice camping pad from friends that I would soon meet, but the only space big enough for it was the small hallway just inside her front door. The apartment was in a very large mock English Tudor house. (The last time I was there, it was no longer a residence, but housed a surfboard shop, a beachwear boutique, and a large bicycle rental and repair center.)

I took a nap—no, not in the doorway, but on her twin bed. Later, we walked around Waikiki, me now in my shorts and a Hawaiian-print shirt, a welcome gift from *Sally-lu* (one of her childhood nicknames). After a long walk along the Ala Wai Canal, which marks the inland border of Waikiki, and around to the beach, I listened with amusement as Sally explained some basics of the Hawaiian language. For example, there are only eight consonants plus the five vowels, and most letters are clearly sounded out.

We ate that night in a favorite restaurant of hers, where she introduced me to Bill and Carol Olson. He was an engineer in a local firm and she a journalist at a Waikiki newspaper. They lived just a couple of blocks from Sally's place, which would come in handy very soon. Carol had a lot of contacts in Honolulu and Waikiki and would soon comp us tickets to various events in bars and clubs.

Early the next morning, Sally went off to work at Coconut Island. To get to work at Coconut Island…she had to take a forty-minute bus ride across Oahu to Kaneohe Bay.

TIME FOR THE BEACH

I got up when Sally did of course, as I was lying in the doorway, but watched TV for a while and, having had breakfast in one of the many small cafes nearby, decided to stroll down to the beach. I had put on my swim trunks and my new shirt and had my beach towel rolled up as I crossed Kalakaua Avenue and stepped down on to Waikiki Beach. It was crowded with dark-tanned male and female bodies.

I had only gone thirty or forty feet when a female voice exclaimed, "Wow, you are pasty white, mister. Here, you'd better use my spray."

I looked down and saw two young female bodies wearing bikinis. They were green—not the girls—the bikinis.

"Thanks," I said, using the spray. "I can't stay on this beach long; I burn badly until I get used to the sun." I handed back the bottle and asked if they were visiting also.

"We're from Guam," said the younger one, "so we practically live on the beaches there. We're just here for the Christmas holidays and then we're on our way back to college in Texas."

The other green bikini was looking away, disinterested. "Oh don't mind her," said the first bikini, "she recently got dumped!"

"Will you just shut up!" said green number two.

"Oh I just got dumped too,", I quickly interjected. They both stared at me. "Here, by United Airlines, just a day ago. I'm from Alaska, so no sun there now."

They both laughed, and I added, "I really can't stay long on the beach here, so I thought I'd take a walk. Isn't there a park farther along here where they sometimes play cricket and rugby?"

"Yes," confirmed the older sister—green number two. "They play a lot of cricket and rugby on Guam, too."

"In that case, would you like to take a walk and show me where the park is?"

"Oh sure," she answered, as she unfolded her long tanned legs and slipped on her beach wrap as she got up.

They were staying in a small B&B in Waikiki and came to the beach almost every day. As I write this some fifty years later, I remember the *Guam Girls*, as they quickly became known, and I also remember their shapely bodies in the green bikinis, *but their names?* No—nothing. The *Guam Girls*, or *GG1* and *GG2*, it is.

We walked on until we came to a large rectangular stone and concrete enclosure built right on the beach. This was the Waikiki War Memorial Natatorium—a large saltwater swimming pool fed by the waves, with lanes at least one hundred yards long. It was here that Duke Kahanamoku, the great surfing and swimming legend, opened the pool in 1927 by diving in accompanied by the tumultuous cheers of more than seven thousand people. Johnny Weissmuller, the *Tarzan* star, also swam there as did many Hollywood 'swimming' stars.

As we stepped over the now worn and uneven entryway to get a better look, Guam Girl 2 grasped my hand and...didn't let go.

A little farther on across the road—we came to Kapiolani Park and...*yes!* There was a cricket match underway between two teams of Pacific Islanders—as it turned out later—Samoans and Tongans. I watched for a while and then noticed there was a practice net farther up the field where the next batsman to go in was having balls bowled to him. I left GG2 sitting on a bench and walked up to the practice net.

A Tongan player threw me a ball. "Do you play? Can you bowl?"

"Yes, to both questions," I replied, and proceeded to bowl to the next batsman for ten minutes or so, until someone was *out in the middle* and he had to go in. He thanked me and I strolled back to GG2, only to find her wiping tears from her cheeks.

"Oh, I know you're delirious with joy at having met me," I quickly offered.

"No, it's silly. I miss him a lot. I even feel guilty holding hands with you!"

I picked her up off the bench and, holding her shoulders, brought her face close and kissed her, her saltiness wet on my lips.

"From now on, I'll hold hands with myself," I joked, and then quickly noticed what they surely have at every cricket match in the world—a tea stand.

"Come on," I said to GG2, "a nice cup of tea is what you need.". At that moment, I felt myself echoing my (and every) British mother's answer to some tears.

We had a *nice cuppa* and then left, walking back via the other side of the park and down on to Kalakaua Ave.

Halfway back, she slid her hand into mine. Then smiling and kissing my cheek, said, "Sorry about that outburst."

"He's not worth it, nobody is for very long!" I mumbled, hopefully.

Back at the beach, we met up with her sister and all three of us swam and bodysurfed in the smaller waves of Waikiki.

"We should go over to Makaha soon. There you can watch world-class bodysurfers on big waves and there's also a section of small waves at one end that we can surf on,", said GG2.

By the time I got back to the apartment, Sally was there and I told her that I'd met two sisters on the beach.

"Two!" she replied in mock disgust. "A *ménage à trois!*"

"No, Sally-lu, I think this is going to be all *p and p*—platonic and pleasant."

And it was.

We became good friends. The Guam Girls, ages nineteen and twenty-one, were excellent dancers, and Sally and I went with them to many bars and clubs, where the girls demonstrated their great prowess, for two blonde *haole* chicks, at the *hula*.

One of the more memorable nights was a visit to Duke Kahanamoku's nightclub, named after him. It was a special night and Carol Olson, the columnist from the Waikiki paper, came up with the tickets for all of us. If memory serves, we were all introduced to *the Duke* himself, who was seated near the entrance. He was by that time an elderly man, but still adored by all in Hawaii. He had won many Olympic medals and even became a Freemason and led many charity drives.

We had good seats in Dukes, and soon after we arrived the *luau* began, with fire-eating male hula dancers strutting among the tables with lighted torches and hula skirts. This was followed by the female hula dancers, whose hip swaying and delicate hand gestures I found captivating, so much so that a couple of times Sally leaned over and said loudly, *Ron, your jaw's hanging open!*

The two Guam Girls seemed less captivated, and when the hula ended the audience was invited up to dance with them. I, of course, found the hip swinging awkward and my hand movements—well, Sally said they resembled me clumsily waving at passing royalty. But the Guam Girls, those two tall blondes from the South Pacific, they cut loose with an exhibition of their own, matching the locals in almost every hip, pelvis, arm, and hand move. I was regretting forming a platonic relationship with GG2, and wondered if I could reverse it!

After a while, a local Hawaiian sidled over to our table.

"Howzit bro? Hey man, where those two haole chicks learn to dance like islanders?"

"Oh," I said, "they're from Guam and learned all the Polynesian dances there as they grew up. They're almost locals."

"Yes sir, man they plenty mo betta!" said the local.

The evening ended with a solo artist singing his regular set with his back-up band. His songs were already on the charts, and we sang along and drank more Mai-Tais. Later, we staggered out of Dukes and wended our way across Waikiki. I'm sure all our heads were swimming with, dare I say it, *tiny bubbles*, and of course, the songs of Hawaii's top pop singer— Don Ho.

As for Duke Kahanamoku, he was then in his late-seventies and not in good health. He passed away near the end of January 1968. His ashes were buried at sea off Waikiki in a large, well-attended ceremony with hundreds of boats, outrigger canoes, and surfers on boards. A bronze statue of him with his arms outstretched now welcomes all to Kuhio Beach in Honolulu.

A Day on Coconut Island

The next day, Sally and I boarded an early bus and headed for her work: Coconut Island—the University of Hawaii's Marine Science Labs in Kaneohe Bay. We crossed Oahu via the main highway and Likelike Pass and alighted in Kaneohe. We walked down through the town to the small dock where the lab's launch was waiting to take staff across to the island. The Hawaiian name for the island is Moku'ole Loele, and yes, it was also the location selected to film most of the outdoor scenes for the hit 1960s TV series, *Gilligan's Island*.

Sally introduced me to most of the staff as soon as we arrived. The one person I remember best was a post-doctoral scientist known by all as *Charlie Shark*. He had studied sharks all over the world and was now at Coconut Island for a year. We got to be good friends and hung out a lot with him and others after work in the Waikiki area.

Sally next took me down to a dock area where several skiffs with motors were tied up. She directed me to the middle seat of one as she jumped down and nimbly started the outboard and cast off.

We headed out into Kaneohe Bay. I had never seen the practical watercraft skills that she now exhibited. With her hair blowing in the breeze, she took me around several small islands in the bay and then we headed out to an isolated sand bar where she beached the boat. We swam and played in the waves and beachcombed for shells and interesting rocks.

We were both far away from all civilization on an idyllic South Pacific atoll when the noise of an aircraft landing at the nearby Marine air base brought us back quickly, if not down to earth, at least to sand and shells. After stopping at another small island with a few trees, we motored back to the lab dock, tied up the skiff, and went inside for a cuppa, before catching the bus across the pass to Waikiki.

The University of Hawaii's Marine Science Laboratory at Coconut Island.

Rude Awakening #1

Landlord

I have had several rude awakenings in my life—alarm clocks, sleeping partners that needed to be taken home *right now*, even a Mayday alarm, but this was quite different.

Sally and I, the Guam Girls, and a large group from Coconut Island on a Friday night had essentially been doing a pub crawl, well a *luau lagniappe* if you will, across Waikiki. So it was that about eight a.m. on Saturday morning I was still sound asleep in my *quarters* on the foam pad positioned in the entryway to Sally's miniature apartment.

Dreaming away of a tropical paradise—*oh no, I was already there*—but dreaming away in any case, my head received a heavy blow as I lay there asleep. I awoke in pain just as a second *incoming* struck close to the same spot.

At this juncture, I jumped up, throwing off the sheet, and yelled, "What the h---!"

A voice in broken English uttered loudly, "You no live here! You, no live here!"

I got it twice just like the two growing lumps on my head.

"I know I don't live here, I'm just visiting. Who the hell are you?"

"This my house," he said. "She my new girlfriend!"

"Don't be stupid," said a voice emerging from the bedroom and attached to Sally, "you're just my landlord…and he's my brother."

And I added, just for complete redundancy, "And she's my sister!"

My tenure at the tiny apartment ended then and there, and Sally's was short-lived due to that incident.

Rude Awakening #2

Surfers

Sally called over to Bill Olson and Carol Johnson's house a couple of blocks away. They laughed at the tale and said, *come on over, though the couch on the 'lanai' may have a couple of lumps of its own.*

It was a beautiful screened-in *lanai* (a porch), with tropical plants and artwork, of course, and the only lumps I found there were the ones I brought with me.

I stayed a couple of weeks there in 1967 on their flower-filled lanai and Sally and I celebrated Christmas and New Year's Eve there also. It was during that time that we met Mick McMenamin, an Irish-American transplant from New Jersey. He had lingered on the beach one day coming out of the water with his surfboard and had stopped to meet me. The fact that the Guam Girls were there lounging on the sand in their bikinis was purely incidental!

"Do you surf?" he asked me.

"Well, couch-surfing right now is all I do," uttering, I believe, one of the first uses of the phrase.

"I have a spare board if you want to borrow it."

"Well, no I can't surf—but I'd like to learn."

"So walk back with me to my apartment and I'll lend it to you."

My first tropical Christmas, at Olson's on Waikiki, 1967.

It was only a couple of blocks to his place, diagonally across the well-kept grass of Fort DeRussy, the military recreation area, and over to Kuamoo Street, number 448, not far from the Ala Wai Canal. I shared a sandwich with Mick, an appropriate food item for the history of the islands named after Lord Sandwich.

Then we headed back to the beach, Mick all the while explaining to me some basics about surfing. "The board is waxed so it is sticky and holds your feet when you stand up. It's a tricky move to master, from lying on the board to crouching to standing; it takes practice. Steering is done with the back foot applying pressure sideways; it causes the fixed rudder called a *skeg* to move the board left or right."

Mick then remembered he had to meet someone farther down the beach. So he took his board and left with the words, "Bring the board back to 448, ok?"

Oh boy was he right. I paddled out, but with difficulty, and it took some balance to do just that. When I eventually reached the area with all the surfers and the usually small but well-shaped Waikiki waves, I turned around and just then a wave came along. I paddled hard and after a while got on one knee, but as I gingerly stood up, everything slid away beneath me and I fell headlong into the water.

The board sped away, however, and surfed itself delicately straight onto the beach (this was way before leashes were invented), where a mother quickly warned her young daughter, *Look out Janie, a surfer's lost his board. Don't get in his way—they're wonderful athletes.* I had body surfed back to the beach in time to hear the word *surfer* and wondered who she was talking about.

I paddled back out and was met by a very unwelcoming welcome committee

"Hey Haole! Whaddya think your doin?"

"Trying to surf," I sputtered back.

"Well, you just stole my wave," said the first of three quite annoyed and increasingly belligerent native Hawaiians.

"And what the hell you doin' with Mick's board, haole?" was the second guy's enquiry.

"Stole? These waves belong to you?"

"Yes," was the triple-voiced reply, "these waves *do* belong to us, but we let you people ride them, too."

The first guy spat heavily into the water—a lot nearer my board than his.

"There's a system in surfing, an ancient honorific order, goddammit—the last one out here waits until all others have caught a wave or gets a signal from others to go ahead. Got it, haole?"

I waited from then on to be the only one left or get a signal to go ahead. I think I made it up once, then started yelling at my feeble success and quickly fell off.

After a while, I made it back to the area where the Guam Girls had been sunning themselves, but they were gone. Nearby sunbathers said they left with two *local* surfers—*Darn!*

Back at 448, an address I learned quickly and obviously remember to this day, Mick offered that Sally and I could stay there in an empty bedroom. There were no beds and little else in there, but he said he could rustle up a couple of camping pads, so that decided it.

I told Sally when she returned from work that day. She smiled with relief, and we went over together and collected her belongings from her *new boyfriend's* apartment. That night after we'd moved in, we took Mick out to eat at a locals bar he knew that gave out sashimi as *pupus* (free bar snacks) and also served two-finger poi (*Funk and Wagnall's time again?*).

The next day we were all at the beach again—Mick, the Guam Girls, and Sally and I. They were soon in a long conversation, so I ventured out into the surf. This time, I had a little trouble paddling and balancing, but made it out. When I did, there were the same three locals resting casually on their boards.

They each nodded in succession, said nothing, but there was no *flying saliva* either. I waited until they and several others had caught waves, really until there was no one within fifty yards of me, before I attempted to catch my own. I caught a few, but struggled the rest of the afternoon—I could crouch ok, but actually standing and staying balanced, *no!*

Later that afternoon, I paddled back out and there were the locals. The first one looked straight at me and said, "Mo-betta, haole, mo betta!"

The second smiled and said, "That's *da-kine.*"

The third just nodded and said, "You got it-bro."

I felt honored and was about to say *aloha* or something like that when the first guy looked over his shoulder and casually remarked, "There's a shark out here now, a large black tip I think. It's cool."

At that moment, I believe my mouth was hanging open down near my shorts. I looked at the three and they all nodded that I could take the next wave.

I was off paddling for my life, then crouching, then…I don't know exactly what I was doing, but the phrase that springs to mind now is one I hear uttered on cable news and radio almost every day—*we could suffer an existential threat!*

Next thing I know is I'm sliding up on the shallows between bathers, grabbing handfuls of sand along with gulps of air, then hurrying with delight onto dry land.

"You trying to create a new style of clumsy surfing?" said Mick, as all the girls chuckled.

"Why?"

"Well, you're all crouched down and twisting your head back over your shoulder every two seconds, as if a big monster was chasing you."

"Oh no, nothing like that. Just making sure I hadn't stolen a wave. It's cool, all cool!"

Rude Awakening #3
Whose Hawaii Is It?

My sister Sally has always been reasonably generous with money, so I didn't notice it at first, but after I'd been there for a couple of weeks, I became aware that if we didn't have free tickets to events from Carol Johnson Olson she would quickly go up and pay wherever we were. There was always a brief conversation and as I realized later—a showing of ID.

We were in the enormous Ala Moana shopping center a short bus ride from Waikiki. I was just looking around and Sally, with her long blonde hair and petite figure, was trying on a few clothes for our planned trip to the *neighbor islands* in a few days. After a while, we got a drink and sat down in a café, where she quickly began to explain to me that the entire Ala Moana center was Japanese or *Mainland*-owned and that the worst thing you could possibly be here in Hawaii was a *haole* –a white or mainland visitor.

"There is very little business in Waikiki that is Hawaiian-owned and that goes for the whole of the state."

She then explained what she was doing when she paid for things. "I live here and work here, so I am a *local*, she said carefully, "and have resident ID. There is a different price for almost everything if you are local and live here." She then uttered a sentence that I picked up then and there and have used many times since: "Can I have the *kamaaina* rate, please?"

She went on to also talk about a growing militant movement of younger native Hawaiians. "You have to be very careful when you go to a popular beach. Make sure that any and all valuables are placed in the trunk before you leave the car. Local elements casually watch the parking lots and when they spot a likely vehicle will simply take a crowbar, force open the trunk, and take what they want."

Queen Liliuokalani of Hawaii was the island kingdom's last monarch. She assumed the throne in 1891 and was overthrown by American sugar planters in 1893 with the help of US Marines.

She went on to elucidate that the nation of Hawaii was essentially stripped of all autonomy when a group of white sugar plantation owners complained to the White House and Congress that their business expansion plans were being seriously hampered by native Hawaiian groups and the Royal Family. A few months later, a flotilla of US Navy ships led by the cruiser *USS Boston* landed troops and then threatened to bomb Honolulu in 1893. The US demanded that Queen Liliuokalani abdicate the throne. There was a stalemate for a few days and then the Queen did just that, relinquishing all control while a company of fully armed US Marines lined up outside, ready to take aim into the Iolani Palace.

Later, the Queen was put on trial for treason, convicted, and sentenced to five years hard labor; however, this was commuted to house arrest for nine months, which she served in the Iolani Palace, the only royal palace in the United States—and now a museum.

Rude Awakening #4
The Sugarcane Fields

A few days later, svelte sister Sally and I flew to the *garden island* of Kauai, beginning our tour of the neighbor islands. We had been encouraged to use only a certain car rental agency, namely Tropical Rent-a-Car, which at that time was a fledgling Hawaiian business.

Nobody will mess with a Tropical car, but all the others—look out! was the general warning. If you are in an Avis or Hertz, they know you are a tourist and you are in for trouble."

We were planning to sleep in the car, one of us in front and one in back; we also each took a small bed sheet so we could pull it over our heads and hide a bit as the sun came up.

We got our car at the Tropical booth at Lihue airport at about 2 p.m. with a kamaaina rate and headed out. The first thing we noticed within a few miles was that there were far fewer golden sandy beaches on Kauai compared with Oahu, but there was plenty of greenery and many palm-lined streets. We drove all over for several hours and after watching the sunset near the water with a bowl of fish soup and local bread decided to drive back up into the center of the island and park probably in some sugarcane fields. We had been advised to use fields and were quite comfortable sleeping in the little car, which saved on having camping gear and camp fees.

We did just that and by 7:30 we were both sipping on some hastily concocted, but delicious, Mai Tais in the pitch dark. I had driven about a hundred yards on a track into a field and parked, far enough away from the main road to avoid any casual observers and by nine o'clock we were tired and sleepy.

It was still dark the next morning when I heard a *tap-tap-tap*. *A bird's beak*, I thought, and turned over. A short time later, another *tap-tap-tap*. We both groaned and buried our heads....

Within five minutes, the tapping grew by what seemed a thousand-fold, the noise creating a cacophony inside the car.

Sally finally sat up with great alarm. "Now what is this for God's sake? Ron, who are these people?"

"People...?" I sleepily replied from under my sheet. "Dunno, but no one's banging directly on my head like in your apartment!"

I eventually turned over and looked up....

In every window, and part of the windshield, was the face and torso of well-muscled native Hawaiians *tap-tap-tapping* long, shiny, and sharp-looking machetes with the back of the blade on the roof of the rent-a-car.

"It might be your landlord in Waikiki looking for you," I rattled off quickly.

"Jesus," said Sally, "if that's him and his posse, I might as well give up now and let him have his way with me!"

"Relax, Sally-lu", I said, and at the same time opening the front door and pushing one of the *machete men* backward.

Just as I was about to engage in a losing argument with a long steel blade, a strong voice from a short distance away requested, "You'll have to move, sir. I can't get my crew to work. This is a private road owned by Alexander and Baldwin."

"Oh, I thought this was Hawaiian Homeland property," I said, knowing it wasn't.

I happily moved our car over and the *tap-tap-tapping crew* climbed up into the back of their truck and eased passed us. They were off to eight laborious hours of cutting and stacking sugarcane—and we were ready for a light breakfast and the beach.

So Sally and I, still sleepy, stepped into the cover of the ten-foot-high sugarcane, fertilized it well, then drove away in the direction of Hanalei Bay.

HANALEI BAY

We drove down out of our *cane fields hotel* then passed by an enormous new development called Princeville. It was big then and has since expanded to about fifty thousand acres of hotels, houses, condos, and apartments. We were glad to leave it behind us and enter a quiet area of lush foliage crowding the two-lane highway.

Hanalei Bay is often said by travel writers to be one of the most beautiful vistas in the world, and the reality of it did not disappoint one bit. The view of the bay itself is obscured as you approach up a long hill. The trees separate as you crest the top and a magical vista presents itself.

This verdant valley with a backdrop of waterfalls and mountains, the oldest of the Hawaiian chain, had, on most days, rainbows gently gracing the hillsides. Several streams coursed through it and on our left the water flow was dotted with well-tended taro patches, a traditional food of Hawaiians. Entirely filling our vision to the right was the majestic blue vision of Hanalei Bay with its deep azure water and waves cascading over each other as they topped the often-shark-filled bay. On the far side of the valley, the road ended at the base of a large volcanic escarpment that dropped almost straight down onto the rocky surf and into great depths of a thousand feet or more—common around the islands.

At the end of the road, there was a small parking lot. Sally and I grabbed our towels and at first ran along the two-mile beach, then played in the shallow surf for a while. It was then that I realized I had forgotten the all-important (especially for me) tube of sunscreen. Leaving Sally lounging on her towel, I began to walk back to the car when I noticed two very attractive bikini-clad Wahines (local Hawaiian girls) standing talking, so I sidled over, as one does, and said, "Hi, how are you guys today?"

No response, so I repeated my greeting....

What I eventually received from the taller one was, "You talking to us? Why man—you got one! You with that blonde haole chick!"

"Oh no, that girl over there is my sister. She lives here and I'm visiting."

"Well, you talk to me you be in big trouble. My boyfriend's surfing out there—he see you talking to me, he come over and

Yes, that's really my sister.

beat you up!" She continued with, "I like haole boys, but he say no."

"Oh really, how strange," I said and voiced with little thought, "too much time alone out there, I suppose."

I excused myself and walked back along the golden sands that were almost vibrating with the heat and grabbed the sunscreen from the car.

On the way back along the beach, only one of the girls was there, but as I approached she quickly offered, "My friend wants to *talk story* with you. She's over there by those trees."

I was still rubbing the aloe cream stuff onto my arms as I passed the trunk of a large palm tree and an arm shot out. I stared at it for a second and then it grabbed my arm and pulled me in closer.

"You got a lot of balls, buddy. You bring a beautiful haole chick to the beach, then leave her and come over to chat us up! Well, you know what I think?"

"You really don't understand..." I began to stammer.

"Well, I love it," she said, "just love it," and pulled me close to her. "Anytime I can exert a little *aloha magic* on a guy and distract him, I feel good."

She had now placed my hand on her waist and was caressing it. My brain is saying *shut up and immerse yourself,* but my mouth is blabbering on with, "She really is my...."

At that moment, the other wahine on the beach calls out, "The guys are back. Kimo's talking to that haole chick—has been for a while...."

Well, you'd thought I'd had the plague! She brushed my hand away like swatting a fly, kicked at some sand, and was gone.

Mr. Kimo saw her too and rapidly curtailed his chat-up with Sally.

When I reached her, all she could say was, "Wow, those guys are smooth talkers. And that glistening body! He said he lives with his brother and there is a spare bedroom if and when I come back here that I could stay in."

We were climbing the hill out of Hanalei as the sunset crashed into the deep and blue ocean waters, followed by the phenomenal green flash, when Sally looked back from the pure romance of the scene and continued about the surfer guy, "Right. He's got two chicks on the beach and he's hustling me. I was born at night, brother Ronan, but it wasn't last night!"

It was then I thought of the Shakespearean line: "Oh what a tangled web we weave, when we do practice to deceive."

After many years of reciting it, I was fully informed by Fairbanks Shakespeare Theatre actors that it was not by the Bard himself at all, but a much later line created by Sir Walter Scott. More deception.

A Visit to Maui

A day or so later, Sally and I flew from Lihue, Kauai to Kahului Airport situated in the narrow *waist* of the Isle of Maui. On the way there, we flew right over the Island of Molokai and its infamous Kalaupaupa Peninsula. On a later visit, I would get the opportunity, with rarely granted permission, to hike down the rugged trail, enter the isolated former leper colony, and meet several residents.

We rented another Tropical Rent-a-Car; they had been serving us well with no *anti-haole* confrontations, despite the cramped sleeping quarters, and from the airport it was only an hour's drive through pineapple and sugarcane fields, then around the narrow coastal road north to Lahaina.

It was a small Hawaiian town then, not much more than a village, and the first object we saw was a giant banyan tree with its large air roots hanging down from the upper branches, and now buried in the ground up to twenty feet away from the trunk. Quite near this grand tree was the main hotel, The Lahaina Inn. It had a parking lot on the ocean side for about twenty cars, so we parked in one corner and looked around at the view.

At the other end of the area, sitting and slightly moving next to the dock, was the most beautiful creature I'd ever seen,

89

The enormous Banyan tree in Lahaina near the Pioneer Hotel.

apart from the two wahines at Hanalei Bay. She was the epitome of desire. I blinked several times and immediately craved her glistening bronzed look; I wanted to be close, so close that my arms ached with yearning just to touch her and draw her into my world....

At that moment, Sally, my new *babe magnet*, called out with, "I'm hungry for something to eat and drink. You can stare at that boat all day long if you wish, brother, I'm going inside."

Inside the inn, there were two things that quickly struck us: The traditional single-wall framing and paneling, and the many pieces of hand-carved koa wood furniture that created the delightful ambiance of an old Hawaiian hostelry.

We ordered some lunch and sat down in the open café that was part of the hotel. I immediately noticed a group of people gathered at the far end around one particular table. At the center sat a medium-sized man exhibiting several involuntary arm and leg movements, and very halting speech. As I remember, this was Jack Ackerman, a very well-known Hawaiian diver who retrieved and marketed large pieces of coral, usually black or pink. He was slowly recovering from a shattering event during a dive in which he contracted the *bends*—suffering from lack of oxygen from an equipment failure at a great depth and then having to surface quickly in order to breathe. Full recovery is still possible after such an event, but one must be placed into a hyperbaric chamber and be brought up to surface air pressure very slowly to remove nitrogen in the bloodstream. On Maui at that time, there was no such chamber available and so recovery was a lot slower.

Later that night, Sally and I were sitting at the bar of the hotel and a young man was engaging her in conversation—*Duh*—when he casually offered that he was *minding* the racing yacht tied to the dock while he awaited the arrival of the new owners.

My head swiveled toward him as I stuttered, "You're in charge of her—the sleek perfect lady gracing the quayside?"

"Er—yes. She's the *Stormalong*, a forty-four-foot racing yacht. She won her class in last year's Trans-Pacific Race from California to Hawaii. I'll show you around her tomorrow if you like. I helped bring her over from Honolulu."

Next morning, we clambered out of our little twelve-foot Datsun car, walked over and had breakfast at the inn, then met

The Pioneer Hotel, built in 1901, is still a famous destination in Lahaina.

Brian the *beauty minder*, who was waiting next to the *Stormalong*. We went aboard and were given the grand tour from *stem to stern*, as they say. He finished off the grand tour with, "I actually don't stay on the boat. I stay at the Lahaina Inn, with the new owner paying the bills. I see you two are sleeping in your car… would you like to stay a few days on the *Stormalong*?

I think you could say it was *nanoseconds* that it took us to decide that *yes* was the word we were looking for—and a few minutes later, we had our gear ensconced in separate cabins on *our private yacht*—a phrase we would utter many times in the next week around Lahaina and the isle of Maui.

Brian did say that when the new owners arrived to pick up the vessel, we would have to leave the vessel…and he added it may be with short notice.

Over the next couple of days, we explored the Lahaina area and then moved on up island a bit to Kaanapali Beach. In those days, it was accessible only by crossing the runway of the local airport that brought the well-heeled to the only hotel and the fabulous beach spread out in a beautiful arc.

The following day, we decided to take a chance on the road that ran all the way around the top of Maui and down to Wailuku, not far from the main airport.

"Oh, you mean the *death highway*?" said several people that we mentioned our trip to.

Be careful it's very narrow—all gravel and with a lot of washouts, said others, *and it's two-way traffic too!*

We were soon beyond the Kaanapali area and the few condo buildings and apartments that were starting to go up. It wasn't long before we were on gravel, just passed Kapalua, I believe. Didn't bother me a bit; I had already been living for eighteen months in Fairbanks, Alaska, where all the outlying roads were gravel, and some, including where we live now—Hawk Road—still are.

There are long narrow valleys that drop down to the sea from mountains more than five thousand feet high in that part

"I'm wet and freezing, Ronan. Let's get back to the *Stormalong.*"

of northwest Maui. Most of the rainfall has to cross the road in a hundred different places. Sometimes it was a wet washout with areas of uneven bare rocks to navigate over; on a few rare occasions, there were culverts under the road, but also many were shallow streams that to be forded in our trusty rent-a-car.

The *ancient adage* Sally pointed out to me quickly was, "Slow down dammit! Come almost to a stop, then onwards at about one mile per hour, brother!"

Of course it worked, and mostly one mph was the right speed to go.

All around us, however, was the striking beauty of Hawaii, from myna birds singing in the Ohia forests above us to black herons waiting in the purple-flowered jacaranda trees in the lower hillsides. The backdrop for all this was a few clouds in the blue sky that graced the east end of the island of Molokai.

We had stopped in one spot briefly for Sally to *spend a penny* in the woods. I heard a slight noise, then Sally's voice. "Is that you, Brother Ron, making that grunting noise?"

"Er—no, I'm sitting in the car, looking quietly at the map. Why?"

The next thing was *Speedy Sally* flying out of the brush and into the car, loudly announcing, "Well, I'm not alone in there!"

Feral pigs, of course, are nowadays a real pest on all the islands. Originally brought by early Polynesians eight hundred years ago, they have multiplied greatly and can even interrupt a *lady at her toilet*.

A few seconds later, about forty feet up the road, a large boar pig, with unfriendly looking tusks, crossed in front of us making noises that, when translated, described that indeed his *daily ritual* had also been disrupted.

It took a couple more hours, but eventually we *resurfaced* on to blacktop and into the town of Wailuku, where we passed several groups of children on the side of the road with garden hoses. It was awhile before we grasped what one of them was calling out to us, "Don't take your rental car back like that, you'll be in trouble—let us rinse it off," which of course we did.

After a full day of slow, bumpy driving we were more content to drive back on the paved road across the narrow isthmus of the island and to our luxury lodgings on the racing yacht *Stormalong*. We went to *our quarters* early.

Just as well, because at about 8 a.m. Brian came quickly aboard and knocked on our cabin doors. "The new owner has just arrived at Kahului Airport; he's renting a car now and will be here in an hour."

We both knew what that meant and within thirty minutes we'd packed up our belongings and tidied up the vessel to a *ship-shape* condition. We thanked Brian effusively for his hospitality and were finishing breakfast at the Lahaina Inn when the new owner and his wife arrived to inspect the yacht. We did not linger but headed out, as we intended to drive to the rim of Mt. Haleakala, the dormant volcano on the other side of Maui, before returning to the airport for a flight to the Big Island.

The drive to Mt. Haleakala was long and tedious; the first half hour or so was fairly easy, but then it started to get narrow and windy as we started upward. Mt. Haleakala is more than ten thousand feet above sea level—and that's about where we began. When the real climbing began, we went back and forth on a series of switchbacks and hairpin turns that seemed endless. There were also buses and small loaded trucks on this same road.

Before we reached the rim, the temperature started to plummet. Both of us added a long-sleeved shirt and closed all the windows. At the top, there was a trail that ran all around the crater—about a five mile hike. We stood and looked at it. It was now freezing cold and the thin air started to affect us—our breathing was now in short, sharp gasps. We did not stay long at the top.

When we started to descend, the reason for the buses and loaded trucks became apparent.

The buses had disgorged more than a hundred people and the trucks had unloaded their bicycles. The excursion was, and still is, to pay for a ride up to the top and freewheel all the way down to the flatlands for almost an hour. The presence of all those bicycles made it a tricky cruise downhill for us. In some areas, the cyclists were five abreast on the roadway, and in others two or three had stopped in the road to assist someone who had fallen off. Once again, driving very slowly and cautiously was required so we didn't cause an accident—or become one.

Our arrival at Kahului Airport was barely on time, but we turned in our rental car and were soon boarding a flight to Hawaii, the Big Island.

FROM DORMANT TO ACTIVE

When in an aircraft you approach the Kailua-Kona Airport from the north, a striking visage is presented to you. For several miles before landing, there is an almost continuous presence of black volcanic lava on both sides of the plane. The coastal highway is a black strip of asphalt within a sea of black rock. This large flow occurred about two hundred years ago and emanated from the last eruption of Mt. Hualalai, the western most active volcano on Hawaii, which created the peninsula on which the Kona International Airport stands. There are two main types of lava; in Hawaiian they are called *A'a* and *Pahoehoe*. A'a is rough, stony, and piled-up in appearance, whereas Pahoehoe is smooth and solid, with a flowing look to it.

The plane landed and, yes, once again we picked up a Tropical Rent-a-Car. We immediately headed back the way we had come in to take a closer look at the lava fields. We stopped at the side of the road and could step straight onto lava. The A'a with its hard, stony finish was almost impossible to walk on and when you slipped and put your hands down, it was sharp, rough, and unyielding. We looked around and found some Pahoehoe; it was smooth with a wrinkled finish, and looked as if it was still flowing—easy to walk on.

We quickly realized that at all the other islands we had visited, active volcanoes were a thing of the past. The Big Island was completely different.

Volcanic activity was everywhere as we drove back south through the small towns of Kailua, Keahou, and a place actually named Captain Cook. We had heard on the car radio that the Kilauea Crater of the Mauna Kea volcano was erupting almost continuously at that time, so we headed in that direction.

In large areas of the south of the island were subdivisions consisting completely of old lava flows. These ten-to-fifteen-acre tracts were quite inexpensive and often had grandiose names like *Royal Hawaiian Estates*, or similar. When we arrived there, it became obvious why. Some of the land had already been inundated by newer lava flows and others appeared imminent. Some houses had survived with the flow going near them and one striking sight was a tiny intact chapel completely encircled by the rough and stony A'a. A cardboard sign had been erected next to the entrance: *Thank you, God* in large letters. It could well have said, *Thank you, Goddess, Madame Pele.* Hawaiians believe strongly in their gods and their control over the natural forces of the islands. There are nowadays several large geothermal power plants generating most of the electricity that the big island needs, but in 1968 there was only one experimental plant and it *generated* a large amount of protest due to the *insult* that was being given to the goddess, Madame Pele.

The air now had a strong odor of burning rocks, vegetation, and occasionally entire houses caught in the path of the unstoppable flows. We drove on and it was another hour or so before we climbed up to the top of Kilauea and found there, in January 1968, only a small official looking building marked, *Volcano Observatory.* There was also a large parking lot, so I drove over to the back of it and parked. It had been dark for a few hours already, so Sally and I laid out the thin foam pads we had acquired and fell asleep in our little car.

And then came *Rude Awakening* Number 5...or is it 6?

Kīlauea in Halema'uma'u Crater, similar to what Sally and I observed.

There came a *rat-a-tat-tat* on the car door window just above my head. It was a familiar sound now, but not pleasant, just like all the others. I pulled back the corner of the sheet and looked up. Sally in back grunted, but gentle, not a wild pig sound, and I quickly said, "Stay there Lulu, I'm sure I'll just have to move the car."

I glanced through the window at a very official looking tan uniform and a large brimmed hat. All this was framing a female face that oddly, was smiling—and it was still dark outside.

"I'll move,", I offered. "Please show me where I can park?"

"Oh, no you're fine, only the volcano is erupting right now. It's actually been generally erupting for about six months, but about an hour ago it commenced a separate large flare-up of red hot lava and we thought that, as you are the only people here other than we rangers and volcanologists, you might want to view it from the edge. I can guide you two over there!"

No further invitation was needed. She waited while we clambered out, then the three of us walked carefully over to near the edge, about four or five feet back, as I remember, where she started to point out various features of the exploding-red cauldron several hundred feet below us.

There was molten rock, *magma*, bubbling at the base, with occasional fiery spurts of liquid lava shooting up a hundred feet or more. Flames shot out of the lava as it rose and then cascaded back down into the pool of liquid magma emanating from deep in the earth.

We were mesmerized and stood there for the best part of an hour until the wind shifted and some acrid smoke started to come our way. It didn't last long, but the park ranger said that she had better get back inside the small observatory and check the recording machine. Sally said she had better get back inside the car and check her *sleeping machine*.

We both went back to sleep quickly and did not wake up early—it was quite comfy in the car. Well, we did have a good heater a few hundred feet away.

We left Kilauea somewhat reluctantly, with the knowledge that Sally and I had been the only visitors from anywhere in the world to witness the previous night's eruption, and drove over to Hilo via H11, the Hawaii Belt Road. It took about an hour. We toured through the attractive town populated mainly by locals. We stopped and walked around the newly paved waterfront area. It had suffered a devastating tsunami tidal wave in 1960, which took the lives of sixty local residents.

Sally took the opportunity, when we spotted a pay phone, to call her lab at Coconut Island. The news from there was not good; the federal grant under which she had been working had been cut back drastically and there were concerns that she could lose her job. We decided then to fly back that night to Oahu from Hilo.

We arrived back at Honolulu at about 6 p.m. and went straight by bus to Waikiki and Mick's apartment at 448, Kuamoo

St., where Sally made several calls to colleagues from the lab in an attempt to clarify what was going on.

The next morning, she hopped on the bus and went over to Kailua and Coconut Island where she heard, firsthand, the bad news. Her job was reduced to one day a week. She picked up her paycheck and in an uncharacteristic fit of discontent—quit.

When she arrived back at 448, I had just returned from surfing—well, stumbling, grasping, and falling—and was able to console her a little. What did *not* console her then was the sentence I uttered—a statement repeated often during our many years in Alaska:

"I've found a better place!"

"Don't be ridiculous!" she snorted. "This is Hawaii… Paradise! Alaska? Not bloody likely!"

The words blew away down the beach on the trade winds, and a week later, via Seattle and more standby tickets, we arrived in Fairbanks in January—and *oh yes*, at -40F!

It's a Dry Cold
and There's No Wind

I made a quick call to an old friend, Dick Swainbank, while the flight to Fairbanks was at the obligatory stop in Anchorage. He was a graduate student from the north of England doing a Ph.D. in geology and mineral prospecting. He said it was quite cold, but his vehicle was running and he would pick us up and take us over to Hess Hall on campus. I had reserved my room before leaving, so still had the key. We also brought the two thin foam pads with us, our comforters from Hawaii.

Dick met us and helped with the luggage as we crossed the road in front of the terminal and found his car quickly in the *park anywhere, no meters, rough gravel* airport parking lot of the sixties. It was only a ten-minute ride to the UAF campus where Dick dropped us off at the dorm door and we agreed to meet him the next day at the SUB nearby.

Sally had said very little once we hit the *big chill* and only now, as we got to the warmth of my second-floor corner room, did she open up some. It was mainly, "Where am I, why am I here, where do I get a bus to Coconut Island?"

I tucked her into my bed and laid the foam pads on my roommate's bed, which was bare, as he, John Ave-Lallemant, was still back east with family for the holidays. I unrolled my old sleeping bag and with the crackle of heat from the old cast iron radiators fending off the minus 40 degrees outside, was soon dreaming of the Guam Girls…or was it the two Hawaiian wahines…I forget.

The next morning, before I was awake, Sally had gone down to the small visitors' bathroom, taken a shower, returned, and made tea for us on my worn, fragile (i.e., dangerous) hotplate and was looking out of one of the windows mumbling, "It's nine o'clock and still pitch dark…."

Awhile later, I went downstairs and rummaged around in the lost and found area and came back with an old Air Force parka and some mittens. They were all size small, hence the reason they was still lying around. With her blue jeans and one of my woolly hats, she was ready for the trek to the SUB—it was about seventy-five feet from the side door of the Hess Hall dorm, so quite doable!

We had coffee in the SUB café that served breakfast and lunch and snacks all day long, and spent the rest of the day visiting most of the buildings in the lower campus. We ran into Dick Swainbank in the Brooks Mining Building and he suggested that Sally should see the marine maps and charts with the ocean *seamounts* at the Institute of Marine Science in the Duckering Building. Dick and I steered Sally to the right floor of the *Duck* and left her to engage with the many walls filled with *nautical stuff* while we went for coffee across campus past the frozen fountain and back to the SUB.

It was quite awhile before Sally joined us, and when she did she arrived with a smile and a handful of papers.

"Yes, quite wonderful, all those charts, and the marine subsurface environments are remarkable—and oh, by the way, I got a job, too! I start in a week or so, working for a Dr. Don Button, and alongside his technician, Betsy."

Well, still wearing borrowed clothes, on day one in Alaska, she landed a job and hadn't even felt the chill of forty below yet.

After Sally stayed in my room a second night, there was a note on my door requesting that I talk to the RA (resident advisor), a guy who got free tuition and board at the university for monitoring the comings and goings of the residents—in this case, of Hess Hall.

I stopped at his room. "Why the note on my door?"

"Oh," he quickly interjected, "it has been reported to me that you have a woman in your room!"

This quickly became the last straw, as it was one of a number of the ongoing misrepresentations of a certain sibling of mine: namely Sally.

"A woman? That is no woman—that is my sister!" I retorted with a moderate level of venom.

"A chick with a full-body tan and long blonde hair, I don't think so!" said the RA.

"Oh really? You may be able to visually ascertain the long blonde hair, but with what instruments are you measuring the full-body tan, may I enquire"?

The upshot of this engagement was, of course, that she had to move out of her digs. It was Dick Swainbank that came to the rescue, again, with, "I think there's a spare bed at 1009."

"Oh, I hope so because it's getting awkward at Hess Hall. We'll both get kicked out!" I added.

"Yes, at 1009 O'Connor Street in Lemeta, off College Road. I've been digging out the basement after the flood for free rent from the owner, a university professor of mine. There's several of us there now: Susan, Maggie, myself, and a couple of others, but I'm sure there is room. She could stay there until she finds an apartment or a cabin.

She stayed there for a few weeks, getting a ride to her job on the campus at the Institute of Marine Science with one of her roommates, until on a date with a certain Paul W. Quist, he offered that he was living in a cabin in Graehl, one of the oldest parts of Fairbanks. In that small compound there was a house with all *mod cons*, and also three dry cabins with a communal bathhouse that had running water, a flush toilet, and sewer system. What more could a person ask for?

The future *Republic of Graehl* was born!

The third cabin, the oldest of the group, and made of hand-notched logs, was occupied by a young French woman named Jacqui. Actually, it was not occupied by her at all—she was living with a University of Alaska scientist, but they were not married. Her parents, back in France, were upset by this in those days and insisted that she *live* somewhere else, hence her cabin. With her permission and understanding, Sally moved into the third cabin at 542 1/2 Second Street, later to become the well-known and dare I say, famous, *R.O.G.*—the Republic of Graehl. But this is four years hence.

Spring Semester at UAF
and another Awakening

My roommate John returned from *back east* and we both settled down to the spring semester. He was on the radio (KUAC) a lot and I was taking English graduate school classes and, of course, the weekly open forum of analysis of new works: the Alaska Writers Workshop.

I was in the SUB one day at a table with Frank Lang, a Canadian from Toronto studying business administration, and Paul Pesika, who later became a counselor. A tall, willowy blonde entered, got a cup of coffee, and looked around for a spare table.

"Over here," I said. "Frank's just leaving."

"No, I'm not," said Frank—not leaving. I slid a chair over from the next table and introduced myself.

Frank quickly followed with, "Hello lovely! What's your name?"

"Hi, I'm Diane Fortier, from Anchorage. I've been going to school down there, but thought I'd try up here in Fairbanks for a year. What are you guys majoring in?"

Frank piped up. "Business administration."

Paul was right behind him. "Psychology."

She turned to me. "And you?"

"Oh, I've been a research technician for more than ten years, but now I'm starting to write."

"Oh no, not another writer. My whole life has been filled with them." Her voice was laden with mild boredom and contempt. "My mother's a writer and my father, Ed, has written for years and is now the editor of the *Alaska Sportsman*.

We had all heard that name. It was the leading monthly magazine relating to all outdoors activities in the state, and soon to change its title to what it's known as today: *Alaska Magazine*.

She quickly became friends with us and our rapidly expanding group.

After a few weeks, she said to me out of the blue, "They're having tryouts for a play. Have you thought of going?"

"No, never," I immediately replied. I couldn't help thinking of my father's career of many summers in England in the early thirties in which he performed at theatres on seaside piers during summer holidays and weekends. He was in many shows for a traveling theatre called See the Point Company. It was run by a man called Victor Mara.

Sometimes they got paid, sometimes they didn't. Dad had the acting bug and did not shake it until he missed several Monday mornings getting back to his job and nearly got the sack.

He was saved—mainly by Mr. Victor Mara himself—who ran off with the leading lady and, *oh yes*, all the takings. The theatre group soon disbanded to my father's dismay—and my mother's abject joy.

Dad would on many occasions say to me: "If you ever get the urge to act on stage—stifle it, son, stifle it! It is the road to rack and ruin."

So other than a *party piece* at family Christmas parties and the like, I had—up until now—stifled it.

The other person who saved my dad was my mom, Rose, who had for years been forced into quick cameo roles when an actress hadn't shown up for that evening's performance. She was forced into playing chamber maids, dowager duchesses, etcetera. The one line she always remembered, when playing a *Lady Godalming*: "That man has lost his trousers—disgusting! Where are the stewards?" We all loved that story when we heard it later as kids, but she just hated all of it—and finally said, *No more.*

Years went by and I never thought about acting, even when Sally and Maddy Berry, with June Ellis's connections, auditioned for various gigs in Hollywood, via the *casting couch*, perhaps, in 1966.

So, back to Fairbanks in that winter of 1968. It was a very cold early February and one night several of us had planned to go to Tommy's Elbow Room downtown on Second Avenue for a beer or three. My VW bug would not start. It was air-cooled, of course, and a couple of other vehicles were *frozen up.*

The group drifted off to their dorms or, God forbid, the library, when Diane said, "The tryouts are tonight for Brecht's *The Caucasian Chalk Circle.* Let's walk over to Schaible Hall and watch for a while. I placidly concurred. *Nothing else to do.*

At that time, Schaible Hall was the main theatre venue on campus, designated as well for large lectures and a well-attended foreign film group once a week.

As we found seats, Diane slipped away…to the ladies' room I assumed. The audition was already underway. Several people whom I knew were sitting below us and awaiting their call for reading: Paul Quist, Maggie Billington, Liz Clarke, Ben Barber, Jim Hadra, Mary Hughes, Jim Bartlett, and many others. The show was directed by a well-known actor, Robin Fowler, who was replacing the experienced and well-liked Lee Salisbury, who was taking a one-year sabbatical with his family in Hawaii.

We sat there for a while as most of the assembled were called one by one to the small stage area. I watched and was mildly critical of several for not speaking up and projecting, for if my father had discouraged acting, he had strongly promoted public speaking and communicating. *Talk to the chap in the back row. Never mind the 'toffs' in the front, they'll hear everything!* was a mantra of his for all of us.

After another twenty minutes or so, I was getting a bit bored, when I heard my name uttered by the director. *Can't be me*, I thought. Must be another Ron Short here. It was called again. I looked at Diane.

She just sheepishly pointed at the stage, softly voicing, "Go on—you're up," and glanced away.

Feeling slightly bewildered, I walked down the well-known, uneven auditorium steps and was handed a script by an assistant. "Read Corporal of the Ironshirts, please!"

So, I did, in a loud projecting voice that I thought the character would use as he suggestively interrogated the peasant girl, Grusha, the heroine—and that my dad would appreciate.

Well, to my surprise, I was cast and played several roles, as we all did in a production that was performed for three nights in Schaible Hall and three at the Alaskaland Theatre. The play by Bertolt Brecht was written in German, set in the Russian Caucasus, and derived from an old Chinese folktale. The New York critics stated that it had rarely been performed successfully in an English translation. It was also described as a combination of Groucho Marx and King Solomon. The overthrow of governments is a stark reminder in today's world that democracy can indeed be in a fragile condition. Brecht even has one of the protagonists say, "Terrible is the temptation to do good!"

The entire cast had an invigorating time performing the play and making lifelong friends that, with a few exceptions, still live in Fairbanks.

Diane Fortier sat through it at least once, but would only say, with a glint in her eye, "There—wasn't that hard was it, and I can tell you enjoyed it, didn't you?"

Which of course I did—immensely. When I informed my dad back in England he said, "Be careful son, don't risk your wealth or livelihood like I did."

MOOSE DROPPING

Well, I was somewhat hooked and have performed in many shows and served on a few boards, as well as being a long-time supporter of theatre in Alaska. But I never over-extended myself to *risk it all*, as they say.

Slightly Creative,
Very Single, and—Broke

There were parties everywhere that semester, especially in the adjacent, unorganized, and some said ungovernable community of College, Alaska. I would run into my sister Sally all over the campus and at some of the parties. She was now a permanent employee at Marine Science and well-respected for her lab experience.

College, just down the hill from the Duckering Building, was a mixed collection of log cabins, small houses, regular family houses, and small businesses tucked in anywhere they'd fit. There were dental offices, diesel fuel sales, and even a dulcimer maker, along with a lot of detritus.

It was at a party one Saturday night in late March of 1968 that I stepped into a small log house that was really only two rooms, a main room with a crackling wood stove and a large kitchen.

There were many interesting people at these sorts of parties, *from lords to layabouts*, as we say. The first thing I observed was two guys who turned out to be writers John Hallum and Ron Rau poring over a sheet of paper with no doubt *bon mots* upon it. The gamut ran from geophysics professors David Stone and Dan Hawkins and their wives, to a young Geophysical Institute laborer/carpenter, Eric Forrer. From a brand-new lawyer in town named Steve Cowper, who would rise to be the Governor of Alaska, to the respected judge and future Chief Justice of the Alaska Supreme Court, Jay Rabinowitz. And myself, soon to become—a laborer.

At this particular gathering, there came out of the kitchen a loud, almost bellowing British-type accent. *No, not mine!* And not quite British, either. It turned out to be an Australian who worked at the university's planning department named Richard Holden. He, his wife Josie, myself, and my dates *du jour* attended several parties that spring. At one, Richard casually asked what I did for money.

"Oh, that," I replied. "Well, I was at a cannery job in Ketchikan last summer, but now I don't know."

"Well, I can get you a good job if you want it, but you'll have to work hard."

"Oh, I'd love it," I said.

"It pays well, too," offered Richard, "nearly six dollars an hour, mate."

Now, at that time all student jobs at the U paid about one dollar an hour, and all technician and lab positions about four. So that was a large increase for me, but I did not realize then what highly repetitive and tiring effort was going to be required.

"It's a laboring job on the new fine arts/library complex on the campus. I can get you hired via a *student request* at the Laborers Union Local 942. Burgess Construction Co. already owes me a favor or two, so should be easy. I'll have it called in on Monday morning, ok?"

My First Union Job

Nearly broke again, I was excited. I was at the union hall on Monday well before *call time* at nine a.m. The hall was located at that time in the basement of the King's Kup restaurant on Noble Street in downtown Fairbanks.

At a minute or so past nine, the dispatch counter door opened and a man whom I later learned was Jim Day called out to fill union laborer jobs around Fairbanks, Ft. Wainwright, Eielson Air Force Base, and in some cases, distant highway jobs where you lived with room and board in a construction camp. It was May and there were many jobs for the summer.

At the end of his list came, "And I have one student request for Burgess Construction Company at the college, working *six nines*—a Ronan Short."

He finished talking as a low mumble of discontent went through the hall—meant for anyone who was slightly bending the rules, and older members considered giving jobs to non-member college kids to be exactly that. However, most of the members were soon exiting the hall quietly via the curved stairway up and out onto Noble St.

I waited at the end of the line, but was soon handed my dispatch as a general laborer at scale compensation.

Jim Day looked at me, but only said, "Report to the office trailer on the site."

I nodded and said "Thank you", just as he added, "You'll be working for *The Hook*, take care!"

The Hook? I thought, *Where are we—in a production of Peter Pan?*

I had a few errands to run, so I did not get back to campus and the Burgess trailer until mid-afternoon. I signed in and briefly met Darrell McBirney Sr., the job superintendent. He told me to report to the labor *shack* at seven a.m. One of the errands I had run was to Big Ray's—*the working man store*—where following a tip, I purchased two pairs of yellow *monkey face* gloves, each having Big Ray's name on the back. They were the standard *de rigeur* gloves for Local 942 members.

At about five to seven the next morning, I walked out of Hess Hall and across the SUB parking lot to the fence enclosing the fine arts jobsite. There was no gate, so I just climbed up and over the six-foot fence and across the work area to the shack. Inside were a dozen or so men sitting hunched over cups of coffee. Mainly silent, one or two nodded at me and then the door opened and everyone got up, grabbed their hard hats and gloves, and filed out.

The man who filed in was The Hook—a certain Chuck Helms. He pointed at the wall with his prosthetic arm with a hook attached. "Grab a number two round point and follow me."

"A number two—what's that?"

"That shovel there, see it has a round point. You're on the clock now—my clock—and all I wanna see is assholes and elbows, got it?"

It took me awhile to *get it*, but I did, and the next couple of weeks were quite a steep learning curve. I was shoveling gravel just deposited by end dump trucks; two or three of us had to spread the ten yards in a couple of minutes, then move to the next area with a new dump in it.

There were no official breaks in the laborers contract, but other unions had them, so when you were working with carpenters, if you were unobtrusive and quiet you could break with them and usually get offered a little coffee from one of their Thermoses.

One day, one of the carpenters said, "Hello Ronnie boy, so you made it out of the *hall.*

It was a friend from the Big I Bar—a certain Austin Smith from Liverpool, England no less, and a sought-after carpenter on any job. For years, whenever I ran into Austin he was always employed, unlike most of the rest of us.

He quickly told me about The Hook. "Yes, he's mean and nasty, but he's like that to everyone and he has to cover a lot of ground here, so a lot of the time he's somewhere else. I try to keep out of his way. I'll be needing a laborer to haul bundles of two-by-fours in a day or two. I'll try and get you. That's not easy work either, but it's a break from shoveling."

Two more tiring weeks went by working six days a week, some of them helping Austin with lumber. The money was great. On a Monday morning, just shoveling away, I saw the backhoe operator talking to The Hook and then pointing to me. *Uh-oh,* I thought. Head down: *assholes and elbows* came to mind.

The operator then walked slowly over to me. "Do you know how to check grade?"

"No, but I bet I could learn quickly." Anything that would get me off of what was known as the *tool of ignorance*—the shovel.

His name was John, last name of Neubauer, and he was to become a long-time friend and, also the owner of the famous Boatel Bar, aka the Sleazy Waterfront Bar.

"I'll show you what we have to do," he said, taking out of his pocket a six-inch-long object. "This is a hand level. Looking through it, you can accurately read the horizontal height on a survey rod above the ground." He showed me quickly how to

The UAF Fine Arts Complex under construction, with the Davis Concert Hall in the foreground, and the library in the back. This was my first job.

use it, then walked over to three I-beams pointing at angles toward each about three or four feet out of the ground.

"I have to dig a hole around these driven pilings six to eight feet deep. There will be about a dozen of these groups of twelve-inch I-beams. They've been installed by the pile driver to a depth of sixty to seventy feet in the ground and are the foundations for the entire complex of the library, the great hall, a theatre, a concert hall, plus the art, English, and music departments."

After explaining all this, John jumped back on his rig and began to excavate. The bucket slowly curved into the ground and came up brimful as he demonstrated his skills. He barely brushed the pilings as the bucket appeared and he swung it up and out of the way. After a while, he called to me to grab a shovel and clean out the space between the piles as it grew larger. I was standing at the edge of the excavation holding the survey rod and getting a nice break from the tool of ignorance.

I quickly retorted, "A shovel? I don't touch those things now; I'm a grade checker."

He grinned and I laughed as I ran and grabbed a tool of ignorance for the brief job compared to the nine-hour slog I'd been doing.

I learned enough in the next two weeks or so to feel competent with the hand level, also called a *p-gun*.

However, sometimes I was back in the hole with the p-gun in my pocket and a shovel in my hands. One day, while concentrating on shoveling, I heard a growling, snuffling noise.

Can't be a bear nor a baby moose—surely not inside the six-foot chain-link fence, I thought.

Then a small wolf-like nose appeared, quickly followed by a human voice, which announced, "Ronan Short!"

"Yes," I replied cautiously.

"I'm Ed Orbeck with Laborers Local 942. You wanna keep working here?"

"Yes, and who's that?" I asked, as I pointed at the bear-moose-wolf monster.

"That's my dog, Snuffy," he allowed. "The point is," he continued, "that by the end of next week you will have four hundred hours on the job, so you are required to join the union and pay the initiation fee or be removed from the jobsite."

This was a fairly standard procedure, so a few days later I complied and paid the fee of a couple hundred dollars.

While all that was occurring, Ron Biggers, an acquaintance, was entering the SUB with a new girlfriend. He ushered her passed the counter and on to the end of the building overlooking the construction site.

"Well, honey, I'll shortly be rolling in it. I have a contact who will soon talk to Lloyd Burgess, the owner of Burgess Construction, who will arrange a call to the laborers hall, and get me the first student request on this multimillion dollar job. I've kept an eye on the site and…wait a minute, who is that over there in a blue hard hat standing next to the backhoe? I don't believe it! Goddamn it. Someone's got my job! I've gotta get to a phone."

It was about a week later that he got his dispatch and showed up on the job. He came right at me—shaking his head—but smiling!

"I've seen you around. How did you pull that off? I've got *juice* all the way up to Lloyd Burgess," he exhorted.

"Well," I replied, also smiling, "maybe my juice goes a little higher."

It was a week or so before Ron spotted Dick Holden and me in Tommy's having a beer and put it all together. We became friends and often worked on the same job. Later, we operated S & B Lumber together, socialized often, and maintained our friendship.

Later, Ron moved off-shore for employment in Saipan, NMI—Northern Mariana Islands, and he still lives there.

I often say that after sixty, one should have separate beds. We—Barbara and I—now have *separate rooms*, and in our winter property, we have the option of *separate houses*. Recently, my wife flew to Mexico City to assist our son-in-law with our two young grandchildren. I announced then that *separate countries* was the perfect situation.

I have recently learned that Ron Biggers has one-upped me again. His partner lives in the Pacific Northwest. So, never mind separate beds, houses or countries—they now live on separate continents!

A Different Job,
a Different Boss

With the grade-checking over on this job, I was shoveling away on one of the lower floors of the fine arts complex when Jim, a new and weasel-like foreman, found me and out of his back pocket pulled out two checks that had my name on them.

"We gotta cut back now," he spat out. "Here's your layoff slip, etcetera.," and turned on his heels and stumbled away, his heavy construction boots wobbling on the uneven gravel as he left the area. I immediately departed the worksite via the six-foot fence and it being a Friday, took a long shower, had a nap, and headed to the Big I.

On the following Monday morning, I went down to the union hall and at the nine o'clock call Jim Day announced many jobs. Near the end of his list was a call for two laborers for Burgess Construction Co. on Airport Road. I took one and a guy called Charlie from Boston took the other. We were instructed to report to the foreman, one Lon Dreka, at the intersection of Airport and Peger Road at noon that day. We both arrived, parked, and were standing on the corner when a pickup truck pulled up.

"Hi, how are you guys today? I'm Lon Dreka. Do you have your dispatch slips?"

We shook hands and handed them over as he smiled and said in a soft voice, "Now this job is spread out over about three miles. We'll start at nine hours a day, but it will soon go to ten, probably." Very good news for us, with more overtime.

He then paused and added, "I'll give you guys jobs to do, and I expect you to do them and not goof off while I'm gone up or down the road, ok?"

I think my mouth was still hanging open at his calm gentility compared to the coarse brutality of the other job. After a couple of hours, he returned and said...quietly, "There's another thing I want to mention. The highway department inspector on this job is a loud and unpleasant person. Do not follow any of his instructions, 'cause he'll have you chopping and changing work sites all over this job. His name is Jack. Just tell him you work for me and if he needs anything to call me on the radio—he knows my call sign. Ok, guys?"

It wasn't an hour before a bright orange State of Alaska Highway Department pickup pulled up next to where we were raking. A gruff voice announced, "Grab your shovels and get in the back. I've got work for you two up by University Avenue."

As I remember it, Charlie and I both said in perfect unison, "We work for Lon Dreka. Call him on the radio!"

The job was a delight, if that can be said of any construction job. The foreman always *asked* us to do tasks, and there was never any shouting and yelling. I mention this now because I had never worked any construction in my life until the cannery in Ketchikan the previous year. My entire eleven years or so of working had all been in research laboratories, as stated earlier in these small books. My earlier positions all required careful handling of glassware, surgical instruments, and electronic devices.

I had several more road jobs around Fairbanks that summer, every one of which was run by courteous foremen, and I realized that I quite liked construction work. It was the duality of working your body in the summer and your mind in the winter. The irony was not lost on me that my first job had been on a fine arts complex, during which there was nothing fine or artsy in their management style.

By the fall of that year, snow, or as we called it, *termination dust*, appeared along with my lay-off slip. I had a few thousand dollars in the bank and was about to sign up for more grad school when a letter arrived from my parents in England. Doug and Rose were both well and had bought a property next to my Aunty Nin (Lily) in Peldon, a small village in Essex, and were planning to build a retirement bungalow.

The more immediate news, however, was that my father was coming to Las Vegas on another lecture tour sponsored by the Animal Care Panel of America. He would be there toward the end of October, at the Stardust Hotel and Casino.

I immediately changed my plans. At the same time, the English travel partner of Jeremy Ainsworth, Mik Crawford, inquired of me as to whether I would like to go on a drive down through Central America to Panama, and perhaps farther. He said he would buy a used van while visiting friends in the Vancouver, B.C. area and we could fit it out at our leisure and drive south. I said that it sounded great and then added my new info about Dad's gig in Las Vegas. He quickly agreed that he would meet up with me in Nevada.

My confidence in him was well-founded; after all, he had driven around the world once already, including driving down from California to Panama, so he also had several contacts with people and places in Central America.

OFF TO SEATTLE...
OOPS, MAKE THAT MEXICO!

I had arranged to take the red eye flight on Pan Am one night in the middle of October of 1968. Many more snowflakes of *departure dust* were now on the ground in Fairbanks and I dusted a few off my Clarks desert boots and strode into the airport. I had not registered at the dorm for the fall semester, but figured I would be back by early January of '69.

I was standing at the counter ready to pay for my standby ticket for a large reduction in the coach price when the airline attendant said, "We have a super special, still on now too. For only fifty dollars more, you can fly from Seattle to Mexico City and back later to several US cities. It's an Olympic special, and most folks are already there since the games started a couple of days ago."

I quickly said yes and paid the extra fare, but still had to wait until the end of the queue for my name to be called before boarding.

In 1968, most flights from Fairbanks stopped in Anchorage on their way south, but Pan Am was a direct flight. I slept almost all the way to Seattle across three seats near the back of the plane. I then waited about three hours at the airport for the eight a.m. flight to Mexico. It was, of course, an international flight after we stopped briefly in LA, so from then on it was free food and drinks all the way—*Ole!*

In Mexico City, I went to a help desk and requested cheap lodgings near the Olympic venue, the University Stadium.

The woman just laughed and said, "Buena suerte, señor," then she carried on talking. But I understood nothing, except soon I caught another word, "quizás" (perhaps). Then, after a few phone calls, she smiled and handed me a slip of paper with an address on it.

"You can take a bus," she said, "it's cheapest. Show this to the driver."

It was a twenty-minute bus ride, and as he stopped at a light, he glanced back at me and pointed down a side street.

"Muchas Gracias," I said loudly, as the creaky bus doors folded shut with a familiar un-lubricated creak. The address was written on the slip of paper.

As I walked down looking for the number, a young girl, about seven, called out from a doorway. "Ola, Señor, su cuarto es aqui! (Hello mister, your room is here!)

She smiled as I turned toward her and then ran back into the house, yelling something to a person who quickly appeared and turned out to be her mother.

She showed me upstairs to a small comfortable room where I stored my backpack and unloaded only my carry-on. I went back down and met her husband and the two daughters and ate dinner with them. As soon as I had eaten, I felt exhausted; I had been traveling since midnight and it was now about eight p.m. Mexico time. I excused myself and went straight up to bed.

It was probably about three a.m. when I awoke with extreme nausea, my head swimming around and my stomach churning. I got up slowly, went down the hall with my hands on the wall. and just made the toilet, my arms caressing the bowl as I vomited repeatedly and noisily for several minutes. Then, as I wiped my mouth off, any control of my rear end was lost. I swung up onto the toilet seat barely in time.

This nauseating and exhausting process was repeated several times. As daylight approached, I was able to grab short periods of sleep in the bed with a plastic bowl from a cupboard by my side.

I had, of course, awoken the whole family with my noise in the bathroom. The wife came into the room and asked if she should she call a doctor.

I just nodded with an almost voiceless, "Si, por favor."

She added that I probably had, *La turista*—the situation where newcomers to a country or area were very sensitive to the effects of various bacteria that locals were immune to.

It was several hours later when the doctor arrived and after using an ancient stethoscope and blood pressure cuff, confirmed my hostesses' suspicion.

"Bottled water, and carefully wipe top after taking cap off," he said slowly, and then uttered another phrase that he must have said fifty times that afternoon: Electrolytes, Mr. Short. You are now very low on electrolytes—sodium and potassium, and others".

He gave me some painkillers and said I should add salt to food, drink lots of juices, eat bananas (but slowly), and consume large volumes of *te de manzanilla de Alemania*. "As much as you can, whenever you can," were the last words I remember him saying.

My hostess paid him with one of my twenty-dollar travelers checks. I stayed in bed all that day and then through the next night drinking copious amounts of the tea that turned out to be German chamomile, which was pleasantly provided, usually by the six- to eight-year-old daughters. One of them carried in a large teapot, the other a banana, then they both left with the empties—giggling—in Spanish, of course.

I had by now missed several days of the Olympics, but I finally ventured out on a bus to the stadium. I had created and was wearing a new invention—the adult diaper for twenty-somethings—with several layers of an old towel stuffed into my underpants. I survived the bus ride and the stadium turnstiles and was standing in the entryway ready to find a seat when a sensation in my nether regions warned me to wait...so I did and then hurried back inside to the toilets.

When I emerged, there were several other British voices talking at the top of the aisle. We got chatting and soon they added, "Well, let's go and sit down in our seats with the girls." I quickly demurred and added that I had *Montezuma's revenge*. They all laughed and said they'd all had it.

A few minutes later, a young lady came back up the steps, looked around at all the people, and then pointing at me, said in a very loud voice, "Are you Ron with the runs?"

I was still trying to get over the embarrassment of her noisy enquiry when I was taken completely with her piercing blue eyes. "Here." she said, and handed me a packet. "It's anti-diarrhea tablets. We've all had it, and these work great. Take a couple and come and join us."

She headed back down the stairs and I was left being stared at by what felt like the entire stadium.

I went back into the toilet area, then realized I couldn't drink the water there, so I bought a beer with a German-sounding name and, after carefully wiping the top, claimed to myself that it was all electrolytes and swallowed two of the pills that *blue eyes* had gifted me. After a while, I ventured gingerly down to my seat near the Brits.

Blue eyes saw me first and yelled, "Here's Ron with the runs." The others all laughed then finally added, "Welcome back, mate."

We watched the semi-finals of the men's 200-meter sprint and following that, several field events including shot put, discus, and high jump. Then came the final of the 200-meter race and the group of Brits that I was now attached to knew all about the young Australian runner Peter Norman, who had only just made the team, but had done well enough in the heats to qualify for the final.

The backdrop to the final was that just before the games there had been large-scale riots in Mexico City protesting

I missed the opening, but got to Mexico for only 50 bucks.

poverty and prejudice against Mexico's indigenous peoples. The riots were put down harshly by military units using automatic weapons and tanks. The government later acknowledged only five deaths, while the papers and the media claimed three thousand.

Among the finalists in the 200-meter race were three Americans, the young Australian, and four others. Of course, it's a sprint and only lasted about twenty seconds. It was won by Tommie Smith with a new world record. Coming second in an exciting finish was the Aussie Peter Norman, and third was John Carlos.

It wasn't until the medal ceremony a little later that the scene we are all familiar with occurred, with Tommie Smith at the top of the podium, wearing a black glove on his right fist, raised high in protest at the police reaction to the riots, but also as a black power salute to America. Next to him and lower with the bronze medal was John Carlos, also with a black power salute—but believe it or not, they only had one pair of black gloves between them, so he had to wear his on the left hand!

Peter Norman also stood on the podium with the others wearing his silver medal, but not saluting. He entirely supported their protest by speaking out later, on the riots and racial equality, but was severely criticized for it for years on his return to Australia.

By the next day, I was feeling much better and I had a good day at the stadium mainly sitting in my seat, which was a big change. The group of Brits—three couples—invited me as we left the stadium to go with them to a big party, which they said would hopefully be attended by many of the athletes. We took buses to a section of the city called Recreo and easily found the house with its loud music filling the neighborhood.

We had bought beer and as we filed inside were met with a cacophony of noise. There was singing in several languages and one room filled with athletes of several races, men with their shirts off, bodies glistening in the soft lighting as they sang their national anthems, tribal chants, and folk songs.

We moved around, drinking beer and toasting everyone we met. In another room, we encountered several tall blonde female athletes. It was a mixture of Polish, German, and Swedish women—runners I was told—who had finished competing. We were soon up and singing and dancing with them. I swear I heard a chorus of, "Why Was He Born So Beautiful," the classic rugby song, led by my new British friends.

After more dancing and drinking, I noticed some objects in the corner of the room. Lying there on the floor was a shiny pile of ribbon and metal—and surprisingly included Olympic medals—several silver and bronze, and at least one gold among them.

They were keeping an eye on them of course, but they had all taken them off as they *got it on* on the dance floor and they had been swinging around on their necks…getting in the way.

A lasting image of the Olympics for me since then has been that wonderful vision of human camaraderie in that house full of partygoers.

The next day, there was one more track and field event that my new friends and I were interested in. The long jump finals were to occur that afternoon and I was fit and ready to jump—

well step slowly and watch anyway. Great Britain had a good contestant in Lynn Davies, the current Olympic champion from Bridgend in Wales. The favorite, however, was Bob Beamon of the USA, and in his first jump he leaped twenty-nine feet, two inches, a remarkable twenty-one inches more than the previous record set by Lynn Davies. Beamon collapsed briefly onto the track area afterward and was incredulous when informed of his feat. His jump and new world record stood for twenty-three years.

That evening, I bade farewell to my new British friends and by the time I got back to my *digs* I felt as if I had been standing for twenty-three years. I realized then, glancing at my diary, that my dad was already in Las Vegas, so the next day I took the bus to the airport and boarded a return flight to *Sin City, USA.*

Leaving to Go South, then Farther South

As I arrived at McCarran airport that October of 1968, I was struck by people standing at the terminal windows and excitedly talking and pointing. I strolled over in time to hear a woman say, "Look, there's two of them right there!"

"Two of what?" I enquired, approaching from behind.

"The secret airplanes. They fly every day from here to a place called Groom Lake. The interesting bit is that they have no markings on them, nothing to identify them at all." Engrossed in what was happening outside and across the runway, she added, "We're all aviation buffs, so we're intrigued by these aircraft and who owns and flies them. They are normally painted white and are turbo-props, but more and more often we are seeing jets."

I was bemused, but walked off, collected my luggage, and took the shuttle bus to the Stardust Hotel and Casino on the Vegas strip. My dad was in his room when I got there and already bemoaning his losses at the roulette table. It was great to see him, and we shook hands warmly and smiled at each other. He had been in New York and Boston delivering lectures and had slept well last night after the long flight and a couple of drinks at one of the bars downstairs.

I reminded him that 'Mik' Crawford had purchased a Dodge van to travel down to Panama in and that he would be arriving any day now. He would sleep in the van for safety, but could he shower in *our* room?

"Fine, of course," he said, "after all, we are the hot water people, aren't we?" alluding to our lives during the war in Hampstead, North London.**

He briefly explained the gambling method he'd learned in London. It was something to do with every time you lost on the roulette wheel, you doubled your bet but stayed with the same color. It was a bit more complicated, but I cannot remember it all now.

We went downstairs after a while and had dinner and drinks. Dad decided he'd try the Chinese bingo game called *Keno*. I said that I'd heard it had the worst chance of winning of any casino game and told him I would take a stroll round the entire casino and look at the girls. It was an hour before I returned and when I did there was a small group gathered in the area I'd left him in. I thought immediately that he'd moved to another seat. No, there were about six tall young waitresses crowding around him.

He winked. "Any luck with the girls, son?"

"Oh, he's so cute," said one. "And what a wonderful accent," marveled another.

I just shook my head and offered, "The old Doug Short magic at work, eh dad?"

"More than that son, look at this." He held out about a thousand dollars in large bills. Three of the girls were Keno runners that picked up your *bingo slips* and returned the money if you won. He had hit a hot streak and had done well. He tipped them all and they drifted back to work. In North London parlance, I hadn't *chatted up* one *bird*—and he'd found six.

The next day while Dad and I were walking along the strip, observing the different places you could lose money in, Mik

** See Vol. 1, "Bomb Dropping."

Crawford was arriving at the back parking lot of the Stardust. By the time we got back, a message was at the front desk. Mik himself was sitting at the nearby bar talking to a waitress. I introduced him to Dad, and they chatted easily about growing up in different areas of London. Dad was from Acton in West London and Mik from the south near Croydon.

Mik's route to Vegas had been to drive across California and join Highway 95 at Tonopah, Nevada. As he drove south, he stopped at various gas stations and small gift shops. As he approached the enormous and off-limits Nevada Test Site on his left, he recalled ongoing stories about very fast jet aircraft being observed in the distance. Rumors had it, and it was later confirmed, that the US was testing two Russian MIG fighters obtained from defections to Israel. These MIG fighters were matched up in dogfights with the top US fighters. It explained the increased activity at McCarran Airport on my arrival.

Dad's lecture was that afternoon in the theatre of the casino and was packed by the time Mik and I walked in. We stood at the back and watched and listened. Some of the slides I had seen before, but many I had not. I marveled at the smooth and engaging way he had of captivating an audience with the subject of breeding and handling of all types of lab animals: *from mice to monkeys*, he would say.

At one point, he looked right at us at the back wall and enunciated clearly for us—and therefore, everyone—to hear him. It reminded me of his teachings about projecting in a theatre production: *Never mind the bloke in the front row, he'll hear everything; concentrate on ensuring the people in the back do, too.*

His lecture ended to great applause and many questions regarding breeding, ethics, and supply. That night, he bought us a slap up dinner at Tony Roma's Steak House, complete with waitresses saying, *Ooh—three guys with great accents!* The bill barely put a dent in Dad's winnings and by the time he left Vegas, the Keno girls were calling him, *The Keno King from England!*

Picture taken by my dad while exploring Fremont Street in Las Vegas.

The next day it was time for Mik and I to leave Vegas and head south toward the Mexico border at Nogales, Arizona. We bade farewell and, by God, I think my dad nearly hugged me! A great and endearing gesture now, but rare and next to unthinkable then.

The phone rang in the room as we were leaving to say there was a message for Mr. Short. Dad had it sent up, so we waited a minute. It was from George and Christine Munro of the *Niche d'Amour* fame in New Jersey.*** They were hoping to see Dad, but he was about to leave and head to yet another lecture at UC Davis in California. They had moved and were living

---

*** See Vol. 3, "Life in Edgewater."

in Phoenix, Arizona with their two children. We explained we were going to Mexico and would in fact be coming through Phoenix the next day.

"Come on down," laughed Christine. "I'll get the spare room ready."

We took our time and pulled into their address in late afternoon. Their house was then on the outskirts of Phoenix, with open desert next door to their lot. Now it's part of a large metropolis.

They knew exactly where the nearest DIY megastore was located. George looked at the inside of the van and nodded. "No problem," he said, in the same Scottish brogue that he'd had in New Jersey. *How do they do that?*

We had a very enjoyable family dinner with them and their children Iain and Susan. The next morning, they were the ones that led the charge to clean everything out of the Dodge Fargo van so we could paint the floor and get ready to build two beds out of two-by-fours and plywood. All these items were purchased at the nearby superstore, plus nails, screws, and several corner brackets.

We built each bunk so that it was six feet-three long and three feet wide. They were raised up off the floor about two and a half feet so that our stuff could fit underneath. There was space at the end so that in wet weather we could use our stove there. The *gangway* between the bunks was about twenty inches. *One at a time, please.* We bought foam pads to fit and fitted sheets to go over them, also a couple of thin blankets each.

By the next day, the two children had romped around on them enough to pronounce them *great*. "Can we go to Mexico with Mik and Ron, too?"

We made our farewells and promised to stay in touch. It was about a five-hour ride to Nogales, Arizona and we pulled into a couple of places on the way for supplies. Mik also began to say things like, *don't buy fruit, drugs, or alcohol here...wait till the other side.*

I just looked incredulously at him. "What do you mean, *good fruit over there?* And drugs? They're not FDA approved in Mexico...."

"Well, fruit here looks perfect all the time and generally tastes bland. Wait until you taste a Mexican orange; they're blotchy red, green with a bit of yellow, and they are delicious!" And he continued, "Most of the drugs in Mexico come from Europe: Germany, the UK, and Switzerland. Or Canada. Those countries have their own standards, some higher that the FDA in the US"

As we exited the US at the border, we were given a brief wave by a guard. They didn't care much who was leaving. Of course, coming in is another matter.

We drove fifty yards or so to the Mexican side, where there was a little more scrutiny before they stamped our British passports with a thirty-day visa and welcomed us with *Bienvenidos a México.*

The air seemed to change and the temperature was rising as we entered into the busy streets of an entirely new country. We were in Latin America and had no idea what awaited us in the coming months....

New Worlds, New Words

The small banner stretched across the street proclaimed, *Welcome to Nogales,* in English and Spanish.

As soon as we approached the center of town, Mik, having had previous experience, said, "It's great to be back here in Mexico. First up, we need a drug store. When, not if, one of us gets the runs, we'll need anti-diarrhea pills."

"Why didn't we get them back there in America?" he asked, rhetorically. "Because back *there* they'd cost us twenty dollars, and over here about two!"

"Yes," I countered, "but what about the quality, and things like FDA approval?"

"What did I tell you about the better standards in Europe? That's where these drugs come from so it's not an issue". He finished talking and pulled right into an empty space outside a white-painted drug store.

"No need to lock the truck right here," he said, "but everywhere we are from now on we lock her up, ok?"

I just nodded, fully aware of my *El cheechako* status.

Inside, the whiteness of the store was almost blinding, and only matched by the sparkling white uniforms and tidy presentation of all the staff. A young female assistant approached me and after *Buenos Días,* there followed an indecipherable barrage of Spanish that left me speechless—now that's a rare event!

I turned to Mik who, smiling, said, "She wants to know how you are and what do you require here today in the Famous Nogales Pharmacy."

He responded to her explaining that we wanted anti-diarrhea pills and some pain pills with codeine in them, just in case of minor injuries. Both of these items would have been prescription-only in the States, but the young assistant politely nodded and picked them up from a nearby shelf and rang them up. It came to about fifteen pesos, a dollar and a half.

We got back into the truck, which we had named *Blue Fargo*, and I asked Mik, "How do you ask for something in Spanish?

"*Tiene*: do you have?"

I already knew some basic words, like hello, good-bye, good morning, and good-bye. He taught me several more expressions, expanding my meager local vocabulary as we drove on through the town. The lessons ended when we entered an open square in central Nogales and there on our right-hand side, lying in the middle of the *zócalo*, was a very large and very dead cart horse. Two stray dogs were biting at the rotting flesh and a million flies swarmed over the entire carcass as passing shoppers gave it a wide berth. The entire street reeked as bodily fluids ran into the gutters, and the odor was palpable inside the truck.

"Why don't they haul it away? Where are the authorities? Who left it there?" I stumbled out with in shock and disbelief.

"Well, my friend...." Mik smiled. "It's all part of the general Latin American dichotomy: you never know quite what you'll find here. Fun, isn't it?"

We drove on and were soon out of town and into the rolling hills of northern Mexico. We had gone about twenty kilometers, now known as *clicks*, when we were flagged down at a permanent-looking barrier and guard post.

"What the hell is this?" I muttered to Mik.

"All over Latin America, governments keep track of the movement of their populations. If large numbers of people start going to a particular city or area for protest or even insurrection, they can send police or troops there."

We showed our British passports with their visas and were quickly ushered through and back on the road.

We camped for two nights by just pulling off at a quiet section of the road, then parking out of the way of any traffic.

For all meals or just tea in those two days, it became apparent that Mik's camping stove was becoming temperamental. It either flared up and gave us some alarm or took ages just to boil water, so we decided to buy a new one at the next large town.

This turned out to be Tequila in Jalisco state, an hour or so west of Guadalajara. We pulled in and filled up with their local liquid, and I don't mean gasoline. They did not have a *tienda* that sold *estufas de campamento,* so we ate lunch at a small restaurant and then left and headed to Guadalajara. As we left town, Mik was driving as we climbed a long winding hill with high hedgerows on both sides. I had the window open with my forearm resting on the door. It was sunny, serene, and pastoral.

Then it became more pastoral, literally. Through a small unseen gap in the hedge to my right came, lurching at speed, an enormous cow. Its shoulders crunched into the radiator grille—and farther. Both of us yelled *expletive deleted* as the

Our Dodge Fargo was less fancy, bright blue, and a former bread truck.

cow's head, large pointed horns, and lolling tongue headed for the wing mirror and my arm.

I stared into two large brown eyes and felt the tongue wash across my forearm, just as I moved it inside the door sill. The horns scraped along the side of the van, like a teenager with a quarter, and then it stumbled across the road and up into the other hedge. Shaken and stirred, the cow was gone.

Mik stopped quickly and we both jumped out to check the damage. Cooling liquid was pouring out of the radiator like tequila from a broken bottle.

We turned the van around on the narrow and thankfully empty hill and cruised, barely idling, back down to the center of Tequila, where, having gotten directions, we parked right outside a shop with the description, *Taller Mecanico* (Mechanic's Workshop) above the doors, just as steam was rising from the engine.

It was getting near dusk and closing time for the shops in Tequila, but the mechanic and his young son took the time to carefully remove the grille and the smashed radiator from the front of the van. The mechanic, his worn and torn clothing reeking of oil and antifreeze, carefully assessed the damage and said that nobody in Tequila could repair it properly, but Guadalajara, an hour away had several larger shops that could do it quite well. He smiled and said he wished he could repair it—he could use the money.

Next morning, we wrapped the radiator in cardboard, and at about ten o'clock I got on a bus to Guadalajara. The bus driver regarded *el gringo* with some suspicion, which increased as a drop of liquid slowly slipped out of the cardboard.

"*Que es esta?*" the driver enquired (what is that?).

With a newly learned phrase, I offered, "Nada, solamente agua!"

He glanced at the clear liquid on the floor of his bus, then nodded.

It was about an hour before we got into the center of Guadalajara and eased to a halt in the main bus station. En route, the bus had picked up women with chickens, men with dogs, kids with faces covered in candy, and three nuns.

The bus driver went to his nearby office to help me find a radiator repair place. It didn't take long before two scruffy boys were seen and heard running through the bus station calling out, *Reparación del radiador aquí!*

I raised my arm smiling, and they came right over. One of them picked up the weighty cardboard bundle and took off!

The other gestured for me to follow him and left. I had to run to catch up with them, and when I did it was several turns through smaller and smaller streets before, finally, we all stopped at a large messy yard with lots of tires on one side and stacks of repaired radiators on the other.

The owner, whose name we learned later, came straight out saying, "gringo radiador?"

"No," I countered with what was becoming an old line, "No hay Gringo, somos ingleses!"

The owner and a third untidy assistant took off the cardboard and looked hard at the bent copper and brass *innards* of the radiator. I tipped the two boys who guided me there with Mexican coins and after a while, the owner, whose name I learned was Jose, said, "Come back in two hours, and two hundred pesos."

Not a bad price, about twenty bucks to fix the *rad*, but I knew I should negotiate when I went back.

I walked back up through the narrow streets, bought lunch in a cantina, and looked for a store that might sell camping stoves—to no avail. I picked up a scrap of paper from the floor of the cantina and began to think about Ogden Nash's poem about cows: "The cow is of the bovine ilk, one end is moo, the other milk."

I laughed as I wrote it down and then began to think about our blue dodge van and the accident. I jotted down a couple follow-on thoughts of my own. The two I remember best:

The bits that hit our truck and how, caused a rebirth, it's now a cow!

and...

The parts that made our truck to rattle, turned our chattel into cattle!

Time flew and I was soon back at Jose's *radiator emporium*. Outside, leaning on a tire, was ours—repaired and tested, also freshly spray-painted black. With my neophyte negotiating skills I arranged a small decrease in the asking price, and Jose then gestured to *cardboard carrying boy* who wrapped the rad again and then walked back with it and me to the bus station.

An hour later, I was back in Tequila, sipping one, as the mechanic and son installed the rad back into the truck.

"Oh, and by the way mate, I've formally named the truck," Mik told me.

"Really?" I asked, with some curiosity. "What is it?"

"*La Vaca Azul.*" And so *the blue cow* was born.

I wish to thank several people for their encouragement, assistance, and patience.

Joey Becerra, my son-in-law, for sowing the seed of this memoir.

Our daughters, Renna Rose Becerra and Allison May Long, for their love and support.

My wife Barbara Rinker Short for all of the above.

My editor, Bryan Tomasovich, for his thoughtful guidance and direction.

Ronan Short was born in London, England soon after the start of World War II. After twenty-three years of an event-filled youth, he emigrated by boat to New York. He made his way via California to Fairbanks, Alaska by 1966. He has worked, taught, married, and raised a family in the Golden Heart City. He and his wife of 40+ years, Barbara Rinker, have two grown daughters and four grandchildren.

CPSIA information can be obtained
at www.ICGtesting.com
Printed in the USA
BVHW050442011221
622871BV00018B/801